Christopher's Book

Crucial Perspectives

And

Reflections

Written by Christopher Paltz

In Loving Memory
of
William & Rosemary O'Brien

Prelude

Christopher's Book is composed of thirteen chapters', each of which has a different subject matter. Therefore, the reader is exposed to a variety of subjects including realistic fiction, analytical narrative, short stories, poetry, quotations, a case study, various injustices with emphasis on the present day holocaust, prescription drugs, dangerous blood practices, education profile, family experiences (including tragedy and love), and so much more!!

I truly hope you enjoy my efforts.

TABLE OF CONTENTS

CHAPTER I

CHRISTOPHER'S QUOTATIONS

The

TRUISM

OF

RESPONSIBILITY

IS

ACCOUNTABILITY

Christopher looks upon accountability as an indicator of the result of our commitment to responsibility.

AT SOME POINT,

NUMBERS HAVE TO BE USED TO TRANSLATE
INTENTIONS…

AND INTENTIONS USED TO TRANSLATE
NUMBERS…

ONLY THEN WILL FINANCIAL CONFUSION
MAKE SENSE…

**Not fully utilizing gifted talent is a sin
and should never be stopped because
of age alone.**

**Entering the last third of our lives
must be the most productive,
if we are to lead life to its fullest...**

The Germans still continue to wage war against humanity, economic this time, as the ignorant and affluent buy four wheel statuses at the cost of African human life.

Before I end,

I cannot help but think of our judgement day by GOD.

A tough pill to swallow, will God forgive us to let millions of beautiful Africans die because of our affluence.

Americans, unlike Nazis, are killing –

     by not acting –

hundreds of millions of people over time out of
     willful negligence.

I must warn Americans that monumental action must be taken to cure Africa or, as in the case of the Nazi's, be cast to hell.

Are we *not placing the Africans in an environmental concentration camp, where inhumane death emanates yearly!!!*

CHAPTER II

SHORT STORIES

Untold Heroes

If someone holds the door for us, we say thank you…

If someone picks up fallen change for us, we say thank you…

If someone complements us, we say thank you…

Is it possible that several million beings have died for us in Wars without even a thank you, on our part…Yes!!! and we have not even thanked them by formal recognition for their deeds.

When our country was expanding westward, it was our heroes who pulled the wagon trains across the wilderness and successfully brought so many families to settle our country's vast lands. Many heroes died in the battles with Indians and were eaten, left for birds, vulturistic animals, or to decay, as the settlers moved onward.

While we do not permit the use of our heroes as food in America, we do ship them to Canada and Mexico where they are killed at the hand of a knife or bullet -- whatever the case may be -- and used for food nationally or exported abroad.

While the French and Swiss, for example, enjoy heroes as part of their regular diet, we should scorn them for doing so!

While persons who chew on the cooked meat of our heroes, in those thankless countries, they fail to consciously link together the importance of new heroes, who unwillingly sacrifice their life for the gratification of a person's pallet, to those heroes whose ancestors served mankind so notably.

It should be known, that when a new hero's eatable parts fill the stomachs of the unappreciable, that the digested meat will pass through a human's body to a most unconscionable burial place.

Today, heroes are also used in a most solemn way. When a President leaves us in the mist of showers of water on the cheek, heroes are there pulling the weight of the world on their shoulders. They bow their heads as a chosen six led the way. To the rear of the caisson, is a caparisoned (ride less) hero, fully saddled with riding boots reversed in the stirrups, as a matter of tradition…

Today, the elite use heroes to chase a little ball up and down a field.

Today, a few enjoy using heroes for excitement, as heroes chase a fox in an insidious way.

Occasionally, thank God, we find a smaller breed of our full grown heroes at a birthday party where children will ride them, and never forget them, as part of their childhood.

Occasionally, thank God, we also find a separate breed of heroes at a Christmas manger scene and petting zoos. They are docile, while children are able to pet them and feed them without a concern to themselves or their parents.

Occasionally, once fully grown, thank God, they leave grazing to be exercised in a wholesome sport of riding, jumping, and galloping at the will of the rider.

I will never forget what your lineage has done for "manKind" over the years. You may be the least appreciated on this planet for your vital contributions, except by a handful of knowledgeable, caring and loving individuals who fully realize what true heroes we have had at hand!!!

I think it is most appropriate at this time, that I cup my hands around my mouth and raise my head to the sky and shout:

THANK YOU!!! Damn it!!! THANK YOU!!!

Heroes of a Different Nature and Beauty

These heroes are really so unique, beautiful and intricate when fully analyzed – so hold on, as we take a trip into history, composition, music, fairs, movement, endangerment, and lasting memories to so many.

There is a co-mingling of ages for enjoyment from early childhood to adults; although, usually in a parent and child combination.

When children see a "complex," it is not unusual for them to jump up and down with the prospects of so much anticipated fun at hand.

Fun, fun, fun started before the Civil War and reached a "golden age" by about the 1930s, when an untold number of complexes were in existence, operational and anchored to the ground. Now, I heard, there are about only 200 left anchored in our country, while a "miniature complex" may be part of a given mobile fair.

Our most artistic heroes are made of wood; hand-created by a master craftsperson and skillfully painted by an equally talented artist. Each wooden hero takes approximately a week from start to finish to create. The colors are astonishing and "made-to-order" for children's excitement. The exterior of the "complex" is also painted with an abundance of color to attract everyone from a distance.

The music is very special for the children and enhances the whole experience of joy. The music is brought forward from a Wurlitzer band organ and is soothing, yet exciting, too. The music also indicates the beginning and end of movement.

As noted before, many of the "complexes" are presently mobile and part of traveling fairs. Usually they are hooked up to the back of a truck and pulled along the roads and highways to a given site. The miniature heroes are a source of income to the owners, and a rewarding experience to them also, as he witnesses so many children and parents with a gleam in his eyes. As a parent, you hold on to the very young with a hug as the hero moves up and down to the sound of a cassette player – an adjunct to the Wurlitzer band organ!

The heroes are three abreast and follow one another in a circle similar to that of an apple pie. As a matter of practice, the outer heroes are even more decretive than their inner colleagues in order to attract spectators. As elaborate as the "complex" is, there are implied cost saving techniques at hand in the construction of this marvel.

If we are not careful, our anchored "complexes" will become an endangered species, left to photographs and memories in our vanishing minds. Hopefully, we can save the anchored "complexes" from extinction, and preserve the fun children and adults enjoy from them. If we look at the past, it appears, our heroes are all but gone due to isolationism and economic reasons, and not the lack of enjoyment derived there from. While the wooden prototypes are in-adamant they justly personify the living heroes preserved in our meadowlands.

Let's join "reigns" and ride all of our heroes, adamant and in-adamant, to a successful future!!!

Raise the Colors and Follow Me!!!

At Antietam the toll of men was beyond belief. Wounded soldiers were cared for by medical personnel, while many were dramatized, and others laid dead. Who was lying next to the wounded or dead soldier was, in many cases, a horse. Often a soldier and the horse assigned to them, would both be killed on the battlefield and lie next to one another with bullets in their bodies as blood secreted to their skin. At this horrible point in time, only the soldier was recognized as a combat hero whether dead or alive.

Just think, on Veterans Day, wouldn't it be most appropriate to, let's say, have three horses (with riders) to lead the parade. Each rider would carry a flag. The middle rider would naturally carry an elevated American flag. The other two flags carried on horseback would be the MIA flag, complemented by the appropriate state flag.

Stepping in "doo-doo" should not be a deterrent from marching in the procession; after all, the horses present are direct <u>descendants of our honorable American Heritage</u>, too.

At the rear of the procession would be three rider-less horses representing the Marines, Air Force and the National Guard. Also rider-less, is a mule and goat which would represent the famous rivalry between the Army and Navy Academies, respectively. Each animal would have a proportionate size insignia blanket on their backs.

If only we could get all veterans to march or ride in autos waving American flags, it would indeed, be a blessing!!!

We must always remember, however, that while we have two heroes present at the parade, <u>only</u> the American Service man and woman are the <u>ultimate heroes of our country... for now and evermore.</u>

THE BAUM SCHOOL OF ART

ALLENTOWN, PA

(LEONARDO'S HORSE)

Photo courtesy of Thomas Malerba.

CHAPTER III

Rx or Pu

Here's a story, sad but true, about a group of consumers, like you and me, collectively known, as the market place.

Let's look at only a few "off the cuff" examples that I cite, and think how this analysis may affect you...

If we look back, most of us will remember, when we had a cold and our mother would go to the drug store and buy us over-the-counter medicine. The medicine was about five or six dollars of which, we took by spoon repeatedly, until the bottle(s) were finished or our cold was over.

A story, sad, but true.

One day, while I was working in my auditing office, I overheard a conversation between the manager and a co-worker of mine. It went something like this... Cathy are you still going to work with us? (She was married with an eight year old son)... Cathy replied, yes Bernie, my son has a disorder and the medication would be way beyond our means if I did not work... Bernie lowered his head and successfully withheld tears and replied, "I understand that Cathy, you are an excellent auditor and are always welcome to work here under my guidance." He stood with a smile on his face, and said "I am trying to get you a promotion based upon your increased skills and professionalism you have demonstrated over the past year."

 Cathy smiled and left the room.

A story, sad, but true.

WAIT A MINUTE, WAIT A MINUTE, WE'RE NOT DONE!!!

When I was an auditor of nursing homes in New Jersey, I personally audited the largest private home in the state — Newark Extended Care Facility (NECF). The facility was a high rise, situated in one of the poorest and most crime-ridden sections of Newark.

NECF was a couple of miles from the interstate and required driving threw roads with deserted buildings, crumbled lots, and the poorest living conditions. Upon arrival to NECF — which was surrounded by a fence with barbered wire on top and a guard — I was "safe." I naturally took notice and still performed my audit.

Within two years, management changed in our office and guess who was assigned to the audit of NECF by themselves --- CATHY!!! The son-of-bitches assigned a woman to be exposed to extremely high risk, without a conscience. Cathy had to travel, by herself, to and from the interstate to access NECF (through the neighborhoods described above). The audit lasted about 4-6 weeks. I learned of this unconscionable assignment, after the fact, and was extremely upset!!

A story, sad, but true.

Back to medication, some people who cannot afford a specific drug(s) have to "settle" for a less effective prescription. In doing so, individuals will lead a life below their ability and potential. Just think, if these individuals were properly medicated they could, in most cases, make significant contributions to themselves and our society. Economical medication — in place of more effective (expensive) ones — is like putting someone into a physical or mental "prison."

A story, sad, but true.

I think we are all aware of the posh drug companies with extraordinary compensation paid to management. More important is the incredible margins (revenue less cost of goods sold) they enjoy at the cost of consumer health and economic sacrifice. In a capitalistic society as ours, businesses must sustain a reasonable profit over the long run to remain viable. Is this the case at hand? Professor Schumpeter indicated that a company will, in many cases, enjoy significant profits (margins) until the profits are "normalized" once a competitor(s) enters the marketplace. This process is known in part as the "business cycle."

The problem with the drug situation is that the <u>entire industry </u>still enjoys lavish margins and the marketplace has not adjusted the drug companies to reasonable margins and profits. Consider this, I was recently told that a drug company, with a proprietary drug, will pay a competitor, who has developed a generic drug, from putting the generic drug in the market place!! Also, can we continue to be told that research and development, while imperative, is why drugs are so expensive?

A story, sad, but true.

Unless you are under Medicare Part D or are fortunate enough to have a prescription plan, you are up the river without a paddle.

A story, sad, but true.

I recently went to my eye doctor with an infection and was prescribed a drug called "TobraDex." The prescription is not a cancer drug or another class of expensive drugs but it suits my example of a <u>very</u> expensive "minor" drug — take a look at the next page and see what I mean!!!

A story, sad, but true.

This analysis is sad, but true.

MFR: ALCON LABORATORIES

SALES PRICE ANALYSIS OF "TOBRA DEX" *

RETAIL PRICE PER 3.5 GRAM NET WT. STERIL $159.99

                                                    (PER TUBE)

RETAIL PRICE PER ONE GRAM $45.71

RETAIL PRICE PER ONE POUND $20,734

RETAIL PRICE PER ONE TON $41,468,000

*(tobramycin and dexamethasone ophthalmic ointment)

THE

AMERICAN RED CROSS

AN EXTERNAL ANALYSIS

CHAPTER IV

(Information contained in Chapter IV was from fiscal year ending June 30, 2012. The year-end of June 30, 2013, data was not available to the public at time of writing.)

The American Red Cross
INDEX
<u>An External Evaluation</u>

THE AMERICAN RED CROSS CHAPTER FORWARD

I believe, based upon my education in accounting and finance, experience as a financial analyst, an auditor and a certified public accountant, that I am qualified to make notable observations and recommendations to the corporate management, and ultimately the beneficiaries and public donors, of the American Red Cross.

My analysis and proposals, are totally independent of any association with the American National Red Cross's governor's; management; employees; volunteers; the audit firm of KPMG, LLP; the U.S. Office of the Audit General; the Department of Justice; the Department of Labor; Political affiliations; or any other parties whatsoever. I am writing this section of my book, as other sections, for enjoyment and self-gratification.

The factual information contained in the American Red Cross chapter is solely derived from public information acquired in the Red Cross's annual Reports, yearly Consolidated Financial Statements, yearly Ombudsman reports, Internet access, yearly federal and state tax returns, professional magazines and limited contact with Red Cross personnel.

The operations of the American National Red Cross are extremely complex because of its extraordinarily large size. To gather a full grasp of the business an individual would have to be <u>knowledgeable</u> in the following areas: wholesome blood management; disaster assessment and relief; prioritizing the disbursement of assets within the United States and globally; working with the armed forces at home and abroad; volunteer relations; fund raising; medicine; disease treatment; a focus on family needs, with particular emphasis on children; employee communications (Red Cross Ombudsman): internal financing; ongoing restructuring of the American Red Cross infrastructure; public relations; independent CPA auditors; CPAs with a concentration in national and international taxes; attorneys with expertise in tax planning, national and international law, humanitarian law, corporate and labor relations law; marketing; cost management; U.S. Senate committee relations; non-profit partnerships; computers; management consultants; internet management; executive and employee compensation; capital budgeting; chapter management; ongoing education; insurance (Bermuda); and believe it or not -- numerous other areas of expertise!!

Clara Barton

Presumably, everyone has heard of Clara Barton and that she founded the American Red Cross. Presented herein, is a brief narrative of her pilgrimage to be one of the most noted women in the nineteenth century.

Clara began her "career" on the battlefields of the United States Civil War. She felt that she was most needed at the actual confrontations in aiding the wounded rather than remaining with medical units at the rear of the columns (often hours or even days away from a fight). She also was not comfortable in Washington, DC when she felt her "calling" was to provide for wounded soldiers on the front lines and to deliver medical supplies as needed. It was during this period of time she became known as the "Angel of the Battlefield."

In 1864 Henry Dunant, founder of the global Red Cross, ideas were negotiated into a treaty known variously as the Geneva Treaty, the Red Cross Treaty, and the Geneva Convention. The Red Cross Treaty of 1864 was ratified by the United States in 1882. Clara Barton and her associates founded the American National Red Cross (American Red Cross) on May 21, 1881. The American Red Cross, now operating as a corporation, formally proposed an amendment to the Geneva Treaty in 1884 calling for expansion of Red Cross relief to include victims of natural disaster. The amendment became known as the "American Amendment" as spearheaded by Clara.

The Red Cross received its congressional charter in 1900, which was revised in 1905. The revised charter is still in effect today with more common adaptations related to the "OMBUDSMAN." It is important to note the purposes of the Red Cross, as stated in the 1905 charter, are to give relief to and serve as a medium of communication between our members of the American armed forces and their families and, in addition, provide national and international disaster relief and mitigation.

As a result of Clara's work in supporting the global Red Cross network, she was awarded German Iron Cross for her relief work in the Franco-Prussian War and the Silver Cross of Imperial Russia for supplies extended during the famine of 1892. Clara

Barton led the American Red Cross for 23 years as president, until her resignation in 1904.

AMERICAN RED CROSS
<u>**INTERNAL CONTROLS FORWARD**</u>

BEFORE WE BEGIN PARTS A AND B OF THIS CHAPTER, PLEASE STUDY THE FOLLOWING...

<u>INTERNAL CONTROL</u>

1) The <u>definition</u> of internal control:

   One such definition is that controls are a process — affected by those charged with governance, management, and other personnel — designed to provide reasonable assurance about the achievement of the entity's objectives with regard to the reliability of financial reporting, effectiveness and efficiency of operations, and compliance with applicable laws and regulations.

   Another definition is: internal control is a system of <u>"checks and balances"</u> which provide the best measures for an organization to control its operations both organizationally and financially.

2) The <u>objectives</u> of internal control, as noted internally by the Red Cross, must also be considered in context of the Parts A and B of this chapter as stated below:

   Governors –

   "The American Red Cross (Red Cross) conducts its business with the highest degree of ethical standards, with members of the Board of Governors (Board) expected to model ethical behavior in their leadership and business transactions. Acting as stewards of donor's dollars and as keepers of an historic public trust, it is essential that the Red Cross properly be the protected and that business decisions and transactions be free from improper conflicts of interest. Conflicts of interest are not unusual in complex businesses like the Red Cross and in the lives of business executives like Red Cross Board members. What is essential is that the Red Cross Board members recognize when a conflict of interest exists and know precisely what steps to take to address it." (American Red Cross, Conflict of Interest Disclosure Questionnaire, p1).

Ombudsman –

The corporate Ombudsman of the American Red Cross is a unit <u>of Red Cross employees</u> who "will act as a neutral and impartial dispute resolution center, to provide confidential and informal assistance to the many internal and external constituents with complaints or concerns about the Red Cross… it will have unfettered access to the entire corporation and all personnel, corporate reports, [and] documents and will report directly to the organization's Chief Executive Officer and on a regular basis to the Audit and Risk Management Committee of the Board of Governors." (American Red Cross Ombudsman Office Charter, Page 1) The Ombudsman's Office also reports annually to the U.S. Congressional Committees of Jurisdiction, etc.

3) It cannot be emphasized enough, that internal controls do not necessarily mean that an individual(s) are not performing their duties properly or without credibility. In addition, the severity of a deficiency in controls does not depend on whether a misstatement has actually occurred; but, the potential for a material risk factor existing which could ultimately affect the benefits given by donors and received by beneficiaries.

4) PARTS A AND B OF THIS CHAPTER PRESENT THE CRITICAL NECESSITY FOR THE RED CROSS TO INTEGRATE <u>INDEPENDENT CONTROLS</u> INTO EXISTING SYSTEMS FOR

BOTH THE BOARD OF DIRECTOR'S AND THE OMBUDSMAN'S OFFICE.

INTERNAL CONTROLS

PART A:

BOARD OF GOVERNORS

The American Red Cross addresses the issue of Internal Controls amongst the Board of Directors, predominantly by use of the "Conflict of Interest Disclosure Questionnaire." Every year a governor is required to complete the questionnaire and return it to the "Board of Governors Office."

Once the questionnaire is returned to the Board of Governors Office, there is a cursory review, by an <u>employee</u>, and then they are sent to the vice-president of investigations, compliance, and ethics (an <u>employee</u>) for review. Basically, the questionnaires are reviewed and only exceptions are noted if they <u>appear</u> on the form. Usually, if there is an exception, the questionnaire is forwarded to the Secretary and General Council (an <u>employee</u>) for review, and if warranted, to the "President & CEO" of the American Red Cross (an <u>employee</u>). The "President and CEO" only reads the exceptions and not all of the questionnaires submitted by governors. The Chairman of the American Red Cross does not receive any questionnaires under the present system, as reported by the Board of Governors office.

At this point, it is time to introduce independent controls in the processing of directors' questionnaires. Please note, that processing of the "Conflict of Interest Disclosure Questionnaire" is presently handled <u>exclusively</u> by American Red Cross <u>employees</u>. A new system of "Checks and Balances" will be instituted by having the questionnaires, after review by the vice president of investigations, compliance and ethics, be forwarded to an <u>independent party for a final review</u> of all submissions (including the Chairman and the "President & CEO").

Due to the quasi alliance, on occasion, between the Federal Government and the American Red Cross, a federal agency would appear appropriate to do the final review. Under the circumstances, the Justice Department <u>or</u> Homeland Security would perform the last review of the questionnaires. Such a review by either <u>agency would provide an incremental insight to the review process that would not otherwise be available.</u>

The review by the vice president of investigation, compliance and ethics would serve as a starting point for the final review. The parameters of the independent review would coincide with the objectives as set forth in the "Conflict of Interest Disclosure Questionnaire." Some of the issues to be addressed, in detail, by the independent reviewer may be the director's past and present business affiliations, work history, background, listing of all stocks, securities directly or constructively owned, disclosure of contracts and contacts — direct and indirect — along the supply and disbursement cycle of the American Red Cross.

Another note of interest is when the new system becomes operational, the objectives of internal control would be satisfied; however, three contingencies would be constant during the year and require moderating. The first contingency is when a new director joins the Board during the year; second, if an existing governor resigns, is terminated or leaves because of their own personal circumstances; and three, if there is a change in the <u>status of a</u> Governor (e.g., assigned to a new committee) as promulgated by the "Conflict of Interest Disclosure" during the course of the year. Any of the three changes in contingencies would require processing a revised questionnaire.

Further, it is advised that the "Conflict of Interest Disclosure Questionnaire" be a requirement to all the individuals in an executive position (for example, the Executive VP, Biomedical Services), and subject to the same independent review as a Governor.

Upon implementation of the "independent reviewer" into the verification process, and the continued efforts extended by the "vice president of investigations, compliance, and ethics" the American Red Cross will be on the track of effectively evaluating "Conflict of Interest Disclosure" information and further meet their goal of conducting "its business with the highest degree of ethical standards."

INTERNAL CONTROLS

PART B:

OFFICE OF THE OMBUDSMAN –

There are many issues to be addressed in regard to the American Red Cross's Office of the Ombudsman. Let's reiterate, to a small extent, with a definition of the Ombudsman: an ombudsman's responsibility is to receive and investigate complaints and to serve as an independent and impartial arbiter in recommending what may be done to satisfy the complainant or in explaining why no action is necessary. Also, as noted in the objectives section, the ombudsman usually has access to all records within a given organization.

My understanding of the American Red Cross ombudsman system is that an individual will file a complaint with a representative of the ombudsman office in hopes of resolving a particular situation that may not otherwise be addressed or given advice upon. An individual's name may or may not be given based upon the complainant's directive. It appears the ombudsman will take the person's name or assign a number to the case, identifying the individual's complaint. An ombudsman's representative (an <u>employee</u> of the Red Cross) will take factual notes on the case under consideration. A "go or no go" decision is made, perhaps without a second opinion, at least on routine cases. Once the case is closed and the respective "standard" form's content is entered into the computer base (unknown to many, except to management) the "hard copy" (paper documents) are then shredded.

Complaints must be recorded in a standardized format, common to all complaints to facilitate computer documentation of the case. Standard categories must be determined in advance to making the system operational. Such categories may include, for example, a complaint's name or ID number, location where the complaint originated from, category of complaint (e.g. discrimination), any additional information required by the complainant, possible recommendations by the ombudsman, and final disposition of the issue(s) at hand, etc.

My proposal is to integrate independent controls over the effectiveness of the Ombudsman's office. One measure, as noted above, is to standardize the recording of complaints throughout the system and in doing so, access to the data base in order to generate numerous management reports under many assumptions and objectives. An independent access to the Ombudsman system should be made periodically (perhaps semi-annually) by representatives from the Department of Labor. Since the Red Cross maintains a quasi-relationship with the United States government, the review of the complaint cases by mitigation and human resources specialists (possibly six specialists for two weeks) would be apt. It is imperative that the Department of Labor's evaluation team have full access to the "population" (all cases) and use random statistical sampling to select cases to be evaluated. The sample would be used to determine the rate of cases that did not meet the standards set by the Ombudsman's office.

One of the main objectives of the Department of Labor "auditors" is to determine the quality and comprehensiveness of handling the complaints. Also, if the handlings of complaints are in accordance with the American Red Cross regulations and labor law.

Use of American Red Cross internal auditors would not necessarily be in the best interests of the Ombudsman's Office. Internal auditors often have inherit limitations in their approach by being employees of the corporation, by being bias of their evaluations, and, most importantly, not having the expertise and experience that the experts from the Department of Labor can afford to give to the American Red Cross.

Finally, it is interesting to note that the American Red Cross management look upon the Ombudsman's office as a means to improve the objectives of the corporation under the guise of processing individual complaints. Also, I have been quoted: "that when complaints are analyzed, trends can, in some cases, be detected and addressed so new policies can be put into effect to offset adverse conditions in a timely manner."

<u>OVERKILL?</u>

ARE MY PROPOSALS AN "OVERKILL"?...
I DO NOT THINK SO.
AFTER READING AND STUDYING PARTS A AND B YOU ARE NOW
IN THE POSITION TO MAKE AN EDUCATED DECISION
ON YOUR OWN.

THE AMERICAN RED CROSS

FDA FINES

BIOMEDICAL SERVICES

$ 47,778,000

for <u>unsafe</u> blood practices...

(2003-2013)

The American Red Cross is subject to regulation by the Federal Drug Administration. Since April 15, 2003, a federal court has granted the FDA the power to impose stiff fines on the American Red Cross for unsafe practices in its blood operations. The FDA fines presented in the following pages are summaries of individual fines on their issue date. Since 2003, the American Red Cross has been subject to fifteen violations in the amount of $47,778,000 as of September 13, 2013. The 2013 "Adverse Determination Letter" is presented in Appendix III.

It is clear to me that the fines are the result of mismanagement and lack of responsibility by Biomedical Services for Quality and Regulation Assurance. Disclosures of the fines in the media, in my opinion, have been inadequate to propagate the impetus for necessary reforms.

The amount of the fines, while not material to the billion dollar structure of American Red Cross, is an indication that a very precarious situation exists. The amount of the fines is an inheritably large amount of money and is a needless waste of Red Cross donations. Most important are the potential unsafe health and life issues at hand.

FDA FINES THE AMERICAN RED CROSS

(BIOMEDICAL SERVICES)

FOR UNSAFE BLOOD OPERATIONS:

SUMMARY –

	FINES
September 2, 2003 --	$518,500
February 6,2004 --	$450,000
April 2,2004 --	$50,350
March 28, 2005 --	$540,000
May 16, 2005 --	$3,407,000
July 27, 2006 --	$718,000
September 7, 2006 --	$4,224,000
November 21,2006 --	$5,740,000
April 4, 2007 --	$54,950
February 6, 2008 --	$4,649,000
June 3,2008 --	$1,668,000
June 17, 2010 – ($6,390,000 + $9,776,000)	$16,166,000
January 13, 2012 --	$9,592,200
TOTAL FDA FINES	**$ 47,778,000**

September 13, 2013 (See Appendix III, page 296)   NONE

FINE DETAILS

Sept. 2, 2003

The FDA fines the Red Cross $518,500 for failure to submit an adequate standard operating procedure to detect, investigate, evaluate, correct and monitor all problems. The FDA points out, for example, that the Red Cross's standard operating procedure only requires the investigation of "certain" problems, not "all."

Fine: $518,500

Feb. 6, 2004

The FDA fines the Red Cross $450,000 for failure to submit an acceptable revision of their problem management procedures. The FDA notes that the revision doesn't include an "adequate risk assessment procedure," is not designed to adequately identify problematic trends, and revealed additional problems that "raise serious questions about its adequacy."

Fine: $450,000

April 2, 2004

The FDA fines the Red Cross $50,350 for failing to locate 47 units of blood or blood components within 72 hours of learning that those blood products were not in their assigned locations.

Fine: $50,350

March 28, 2005

The FDA fines the Red Cross $540,000 for not following written procedures and failing to thoroughly investigate unexplained discrepancies. In one case, these failures led to the distribution of ten units of blood that were originally quarantined and should have been destroyed because of storage temperature deviations.

Fine: $540,000

May 16, 2005

The FDA fines the Red Cross $3,407,000 for distributing 9,946 unsuitable blood components, such as plasma, that could have harmed patients. The Red Cross later recalled the components.

Fine: $3,407,000

July 27, 2006

The FDA fines the Red Cross $718,000 for failing to thoroughly investigate and correct an employee's record that indicated she had been trained in twelve blood collection tasks, even though she had only been trained in seven. One of the tasks she performed without training, if done improperly, could have led to blood mix-ups and posed a significant health risk to both donors and recipients.

Fine: $718,000

September 7, 2006

The FDA fines the Red Cross $4,224,000 for distributing 12,233 unsuitable blood components, such as plasma, that could have harmed patients. The FDA fined the Red Cross a year earlier for almost the exact same violation.

Fine: $4,224,000

November 21, 2006

The FDA fines the Red Cross $5,740,000 for 207 deviations from the organization's problem management procedures. Those included failures to investigate inventory problems like misplaced blood units, problems with donor screening, and failures to control improperly manufactured blood components.

Fine: $5,740,000

April 4, 2007

The FDA fines the Red Cross $54,950 for failing to locate 200 units of blood or blood components within 72 hours of learning that those blood products were not in their assigned locations.

Fine: $54,950

Feb. 6, 2008

The FDA fines the Red Cross $4,649,000 for distributing 4,094 unsuitable blood components, such as plasma, that could have harmed patients. The FDA fined the Red Cross three years and two years earlier for almost the exact same violation.

Fine: $4,649,000

June 3, 2008

The FDA fines Red Cross $1,668,000 for distributing blood units without reviewing their records beforehand and failing to thoroughly investigate <u>recurring distribution problems.</u>

Fine: $1,668,000

June 17, 2010

The FDA fines the Red Cross $9,776,000 for distributing 7,359 unsuitable blood components, such as plasma, that could have harmed patients. <u>The FDA fined the Red Cross five years, four years, and two years earlier for almost the exact same violation.</u>

Fine: $9,776,000

The same day, the FDA also fines the Red Cross $6,390,000 for failure to take adequate steps to prevent problems such as the distribution of suspect blood and failure to quickly and thoroughly investigate problems such as unsafe "overweight" blood units (which are more likely to develop dangerous blood clots).

Fine: $6,390,000

(Combined Fine = <u>$16,166,000</u>)

Jan. 13, 2012

The FDA fines the Red Cross $9,592,200 <u>for failures in management and quality assessment</u>, understaffing, a backlog of 18,000 donor management cases, and an inadequate National Donor Deferral Register (a list of all people who should not donate blood).

Fine: $9,592,200

(Source: Pro Republic, 2/2/12 by Lena Groeger)

Sept. 13, 2013

The FDA issued an Adverse Determination Letter. Primary issue is Duplicate Donor Records. No fine was levied (See Appendix III, page 296).

Also, refer to pages 1, 2, 27, 28, 29 of <u>"Adverse Determination Letter,"</u> dated January 13, 2012 – following this page.

DEPARTMENT OF HEALTH AND HUMAN SERVICES

Food and Drug Administration
Baltimore District Office
Central Region
6000 Metro Drive, Suite 101
Baltimore, MD 21215
Telephone: (410) 779-5455
FAX: (410) 779-5707

January 13, 2012

ADVERSE DETERMINATION LETTER

BY FACSIMILE AND CERTIFIED MAIL
RETURN RECEIPT REQUESTED

Mr. J. Chris Hrouda
Executive Vice President
Biomedical Services
American National Red Cross
2025 E Street, N.W.
Washington, D.C. 20006

RE: *United States v. American National Red Cross*, Civil Action No. 93-0949 (JGP)

Dear Mr. Hrouda:

From April through October 2010, United States Food and Drug Administration (FDA) investigators inspected sixteen American National Red Cross (ARC) Blood Services facilities and observed significant violations of the law, regulations, and the Amended Consent Decree of Permanent Injunction, entered on April 15, 2003 (Decree). At the conclusion of each inspection, the investigators issued Forms FDA 483, Inspectional Observations (FDA 483), attached hereto (Attachment A). FDA is now, pursuant to paragraph VIII of the Decree, notifying ARC of its determination that ARC has violated the Federal Food, Drug, and Cosmetic Act, FDA regulations, and the Decree, specifically 21 U.S.C. § 351(a)(2)(B), paragraphs IV.A., IV.B.1, IV.B.10, and XIX of the Decree and Title 21, CFR § 210- 211 and § 600-680.

The 2010 inspections cited herein were conducted at the following ARC facilities on the following dates:

Badger Hawkeye Region, 4860 Sheboygan Avenue, Madison, WI, 4/5-23/10
Great Lakes Region, 1800 East Grand River Avenue, Lansing, MI, 4/5-27/10
Penn Jersey Region, 700 Spring Garden Street, Philadelphia, PA, 5/24/10 - 6/4/10
Connecticut Region, 209 Farmington Avenue, Farmington, CT, 5/4/10 - 6/15/10
Detroit National Testing Laboratory, 100 Eliot Street, Detroit, MI, 5/25/10 - 6/16/10
Indiana-Ohio Region, 1212 East California Road, Ft. Wayne, IN, 7/12-21/10
Southwest Region, 10151 East 11th Street, Tulsa, OK, 7/26/10 - 8/9/10
Appalachian Region, 352 Church Avenue, SW, Roanoke, VA, 8/3-13/10
Heart of America Region, 405 West John H. Gwynn Jr. Avenue, Peoria, IL, 6/21/10 - 8/18/10

Page 2 – Mr. J. Chris Hrouda

Northern California Region, Fixed Collections/Distribution Site, 2731 North First Street, San Jose, CA, 9/7-13/10
Arizona Region, Broadway Fixed Collection Site, 7139 East Broadway Blvd., Tucson, AZ, 9/7-15/10
Northern Ohio Region, 3747 Euclid Avenue, Cleveland, OH, 8/27/10 - 9/23/10
Southern California Region, 100 Red Cross Circle, Pomona, CA, 8/9/10 - 9/24/10
Greater Alleghenies Region, 250 Jari Drive, Johnstown, PA, 9/7-24/10
Southeastern Michigan Region, 100 Mack Avenue, Detroit, MI, 8/24/10 - 9/27/10
Donor and Client Support Center, 700 Spring Garden Street, Philadelphia, PA, 9/2/10 - 10/29/10

The Decree requires ARC to establish and properly implement appropriate quality assurance (QA) and quality control (QC) measures. Proper QA and QC programs by blood establishments include measures to prevent, detect, investigate, evaluate, and correct errors. The goals of these programs include preventing the distribution of unsuitable blood products, and preventing the causes of recurrent problems. The proper implementation of a strong QA program is essential to ensure the safety of the nation's blood supply.

Decree paragraph IV requires ARC to "establish, implement, and continuously maintain adequate methods, facilities, systems, and controls to ensure that *ARC* does not collect, manufacture, process, pack, hold, or distribute any article of drug as defined in 21 U.S.C. § 321(g), including any article of *blood, blood component*, or other biological product as defined in 42 U.S.C. § 262, that is adulterated, within the meaning of 21 U.S.C. § 351(a)(2)(B); misbranded, within the meaning of 21 U.S.C. § 352(a) or 42 U.S.C. § 262(b); or otherwise in violation of the *FD&C Act*, the *PHS Act*, and regulations promulgated thereunder, including, but not limited to, 21 C.F.R. Parts 210-211 and Parts 600-680." ARC is also required to "take steps necessary to ensure continuous compliance with this Order, *the law*, and *ARC SOPs*..." and "establish, document, and continuously maintain managerial control over training and quality assurance in all *regions* and *laboratories*." Decree paragraph IV.A.1. & 2. ARC is also required to appoint a director of quality assurance who shall "prepare and submit quarterly quality assurance reports in writing to *ARC senior management* and *ARC Biomedical Services senior management*...that completely and accurately: (i) describe the steps that have been and will be taken, with specific dates for implementation of each step, to establish, implement, and continuously maintain the *QA/QC program*; and (ii) describe all unresolved *potential system (systemic) problems, system (systemic) problems*, and *trends* and their corrective action status; and (iii) assess whether ARC is in compliance with *the law, ARC SOPs*, and this Order." Decree paragraph IV.A.2.[1]

See details of violations in preceding FDA FINES for UNSAFE BLOOD OPERATIONS section. We are now skipping pages 3-26 and picking back up at page 27.

10.a-g	GMP: Failure to Maintain and/or Follow Written Procedures	375 days *[9/2/10 (date FDA 482 issued to the Philadelphia DCSC) back to 12/6/09 = 270 days; 9/2/10 to 12/15/10 (date of ARC's FDA 483 response) = 105 days; 270 days + 105 days = 375 days]*	$1,600	$600,000
11.a-d	GMP: Inadequate Training	357 days *[9/17/09 (earliest date investigator noted personnel without medical training were permitted to review adverse donor reactions) to 9/8/10 (date of ARC's FDA 483 response) = 356 days]*	$1,600	$571,200
12	GMP: Inadequate Recordkeeping	278 days *[1/31/10 date of earliest report of potential duplicate donors) to 9/8/10 (date of ARC's FDA 483 response) = 356 days]*	$1,600	$444,800
	TOTAL			$9,592,200

In arriving at this penalty amount, we have taken the following facts into account:

First, as noted above, proper QA programs by blood establishments are essential to ensure the safety of donors and the nation's blood supply by properly and promptly investigating and addressing unsafe practices and procedures; preventing the collection, manufacture, processing, packing, holding, and distribution of unsuitable blood and blood components; and identifying and effectively fixing the causes of recurrent problems. Many of the violations discussed in this letter, when not suitably addressed and corrected, implicate these concerns.

Second, during the period 10/1/09 to 12/1/10, FDA completed 42 inspections of ARC regions, National Testing Laboratories, and the DCSC facility. Of those inspections, FDA has classified nine as Official Action Indicated (OAI) and 19 as Voluntary Action Indicated; one has not yet been classified. This is the highest proportion of OAI inspections of ARC facilities since ARC entered the Amended Consent Decree of Permanent Injunction on April 15, 2003.

Third, many of the violations recounted in this letter are virtually identical to violations charged in previous ADLs. ARC has known of these continuing problems and has failed to take adequate steps to correct them.

Fourth, ARC's Biomedical Services senior management knew or should have had full knowledge of the extent of the continuous and serious violations regarding the DCSC consolidation and the lapses in QA throughout the ARC facilities no later than October 2008 when the first internal audit of the Philadelphia DCSC occurred. (See paragraph IV.B.3 which requires internal audits to be performed and results to be reported to ARC Biomedical Services senior management.) In addition, ARC held periodic senior management meetings, QCOC meetings, and Board of Governor meetings in which the DCSC consolidation project was discussed. Quarterly and annual QA and training reports were also submitted to ARC's Biomedical Services senior management. (See paragraph IV.A.2.b. and e.) As ARC acknowledged, it "did not effectively manage consolidation of the donor management functions into the DCSC" and the methods it used to oversee the consolidation and operations of the DCSC "proved to be inadequate." (12/15/10 response to the Philadelphia DCSC FDA 483.)

You should note that we have charged a higher per diem rate for the violations related to management oversight and QA to highlight the need for ARC Biomedical Services senior management to accept greater accountability and responsibility with respect to the correction and prevention of QA problems, as well as a higher per diem rate for the substantial and recurring problem management violations.

Under the Decree, FDA could have assessed penalties under alternative schedules that would have resulted in greater fines. For example, under paragraph IX.A., FDA could have penalized ARC "up to $10,000 for each violation _and_ for each day described in FDA's [ADL]." (Emphasis added.) Second, under paragraph IX.F.4 of the Decree, FDA could have penalized ARC not only for the initial violations of each line employee but also for each subsequent ARC failure to detect and correct the violations (e.g., by downstream supervisors and BHQ). Finally, the Decree authorizes a per diem maximum fine of $10,000, and, as shown in the chart above, FDA has chosen smaller per diem amounts. Please note that, in future ADLs, we may choose one of these alternate methods of calculating the fine, or we may assess a different per diem amount, including the maximum allowed under the Decree, for violations similar to the ones listed in this ADL.

As provided in the Decree, if ARC agrees with this adverse determination, it shall within 20 days of receipt of this letter, notify FDA of its intent to come into compliance with the Decree and submit a plan to do so. If ARC disagrees with FDA's adverse determination, it shall respond in writing within 20 days of receipt of this letter, explaining its reason for disagreeing with FDA's determination. Your response must be submitted to me at the Food and Drug Administration, Baltimore District Office, 6000 Metro Drive, Suite 101, Baltimore, Maryland 21215, with a copy to Karen Midthun, M.D., Director, Center for Biologics Evaluation and Research, 1401 Rockville Pike, Suite 200 N, Rockville, Maryland 20852.

Sincerely yours,

Evelyn Bonnin
Director, Baltimore District

Enclosures

cc: Gail J. McGovern
President and CEO
American National Red Cross
2025 E Street, N.W.
Washington, D.C. 20006

Kathryn Waldman
Senior Vice President for Quality
   and Regulatory Affairs
American National Red Cross
2025 E Street, N.W.
Washington, D.C. 20006

Mary Elcano
General Counsel
American National Red Cross
2025 E Street, N.W.
Washington, D.C. 20006

Bonnie McElveen-Hunter
Chairman, Board of Governors
American National Red Cross
2025 E Street, N.W.
Washington, D.C. 20006

Biomedical Services Commentary

It is clear from the preceding Biomedical Services fine analysis that <u>concern for human life and well-being is secondary, as indicated by the continuous fines levied by the Federal Drug Administration. While some of the fines are very similar, over several years, the handling of the blood process has become extremely precarious and must be corrected. Since the FDA has the authority to issue fines, it is apparent, they are not in the position to enforce the causes of the fines.</u> Who is responsible for this reckless mismanagement — the board of Governors, "President & CEO" (overseer of Biomedical Quality Assurance), the management of Biomedical Services, and the Federal Drug Administration.

It is important to note, that the Biomedical Services has "launched" a highly technological system called BioArch. The system is in its infancy and will require comprehensive changes in the entire processing of blood; for example, eliminating the present computer system, to a wireless one. In doing so certain critical documentation may be lost or lend itself to inaccurate accountability — <u>these new systems may not be appropriate for the processing of blood at this particular point in time</u> — remember this "experiment" deals with human lives and human illness! In addition, who is going to finance this new system -— more "bail-outs" by the American taxpayers? Hopefully, it is not too late to fix the current system, and plan for a new affordable system in due course! If the BioArch system is to be implemented, the <u>NEW MANAGEMENT</u> of Biomedical Services must use the utmost care in planning and executing the technology needed to operate the processing of blood successfully. <u>I suggest that it is imperative that the American Red Cross work "hand– in-hand" with the Federal Drug Administration in order to promulgate the safest methods of processing blood and also eliminate the need for current and future fines by the FDA. The elimination of paying FDA fines will, in effect, finance part of the new systems.</u>

Another perspective on the Biomedical issues… would American Red Cross donors continue to donate hard earned money to a non-profit corporation who incurs $47,778,000 in mismanagement fines by the FDA? In addition to the fine issue, is the fact that 9% of donations are allocated to administrative costs (12% in the Japanese earthquake situation according to ***Philanthropy News Digest****, "Red Cross Contributions to Japan Tsunami Relief Efforts Reach $260 Million,"* August 24, 2011). The $1,000,000 donation by Sandra Bullock, for example, towards the Japanese earthquake victims was subject to administrative fees of $120,000. Both fines and administrative overhead are in dire need of attention. Well thought out solutions by new management's perspectives and policy decisions are needed. The status quo is entirely unacceptable in terms of human health, life, and financing as I have presented thus far in this chapter.

CHAIRMAN

Board of Governors

The Chairman of the American National Red Cross (American Red Cross) is a position that is appointed by the President of the United States and does not receive remuneration. Currently, the position is held by Bonnie McElveen – Hunter, former U.S. Ambassador to Finland, and the CEO and owner of Pace Communications, Inc., the largest private custom publishing company in the United States. According to 2012 IRS form 990, page 7, Ms. McElveen-Hunter works approximately 15 hours a week on Red Cross related matters, and presumably 25 hours (on average) on managing her private corporation, Pace Communications.

It appears, that the position "Chairman of the Board" would require an individual to <u>work full-time</u> devoting their entire executive talents, in formulating directives needed to manage a more effective company. Utilization of talent between the Chairman and the President would be needed to maximize managerial efforts to the fullest. New job descriptions for the Chairman and the President would be necessary to effectuate the best working relation between the two functions. The title "CEO" would be eliminated, leaving the operational title of "President" as second in authority.

Traditionally, the Chairman of the Board concerns him/herself with policy decisions. At one point, the new Chairman would address developing the concept of working for the American Red Cross as the most prestigious and satisfying position one could attain in life, no matter what level an employee has attained. The Chairman would not limit him/herself to policy decisions alone. A "hands-on" approach to managing the American Red Cross would lead other executives to follow suit. Further, the Chairman may want to survey disasters like "Hurricane Sandy" by helicopter, give realistic evaluations of distributing assets by personal evaluations and that of his management team for disasters. He would constantly adjust his personal goals to coincide with that of the American Red Cross and its constituents. Perhaps he would attend a Red Cross bingo game for some extra pocket money. In other words, a true leader!

It is apparent from this analysis that Ms. Bonnie McElveen-Hunter should pass the "baton" to an individual most worthy of the full-time diligence of the position.

Further, Ms. McElveen–Hunter was made aware, by fax and certified mail, of <u>FDA Fines</u> to the American Red Cross – see page 29 of Adverse Determination Letter located on page 50 of this book.

THE AMERICAN RED CROSS

Executive Compensation Commentaries & Surveys:

EXAMPLES
1) Ms. Gail McGovern – President and CEO
2) Mr. Gilmore – President of Biomedical Services
3) Mr. Hrounda – Executive Vice President of Biomedical Services
4) Ms. O'Neill – Division VP, Biomedical Services
5) Mr. Brown – Division VP, Biomedical Services
6) Ms. Elcano – General Council/ Secretary

Note: All my compensations presented are subject to President Obama's wage guidelines as discussed in "Obama's Bandaide" segment (page 89).

NARRATIVES

1) "President & CEO"

Compensation for the "President & CEO" has been surrounded by controversy. Let's start with the determination of salary. Compensation is determined, in part, by analyzing other "President & CEOs" with comparable organizations – assets, personnel, revenues, etc. to that of the American Red Cross. The Board's "Compensation and Management Development Committee" would recommend compensation based on similar organizations and would propose compensation based on comparable statistics. It appears that the granting of bonuses, other taxable benefits, deferred compensation, etc., were also presented for approval by the compensation committee and typically, approved without debate.

At this point, please refer to Exhibit I, Pages 62-63 for the position of "President & CEO." Compensation for 2008 was for about a week, when Ms. McGovern was first appointed as "President & CEO." In 2009 base remuneration included a sign-on incentive of $65,000. In addition, The American Red Cross paid $161,867 in other taxable benefits for 2009 of which $136,615 was in closing costs and relocation assistance. It is not widely known that in 2010 payment of $473,570 was also for Ms. McGovern's moving expenses from Boston to Washington, D.C. (Source: IRS tax form 990). Therefore, total moving expenses, as reported in 2009 and 2010 is $610,185! Total compensation, as noted in attached IRS form 990 for 2010, located on the next page was $1,032,022.

It has been reported that Ms. McGovern has contributed $175,000 back to the American Red Cross as a "donation." It appears that she did this in order to shift attention away from her lavish compensation as noted in Exhibit I. Why would someone accept such an abundant compensation, only to give some back? Ms. McGovern would also get a personal IRS tax deduction for the "donation." Gregory vs. Helvering 293 U.S. 456 (1935) is one of the most famous tax cases in history. In this case an individual did everything according to existing tax law at the time. The Supreme Court ruled that "substance vs. form" was to be the overriding factor, not the law alone. Will IRS consider the total tax transactions as a whole? Therefore, considering the $175,000 charitable contributions, offset by income, as a tax sham?

53-0196605

Part II Officers, Directors, Trustees, Key Employees, and Highest Compensated Employees. Use Schedule J-1 if additional space is needed.

For each individual whose compensation must be reported in Schedule J, report compensation from the organization on row (i) and from related organizations, described in the instructions, on row (ii). Do not list any individuals that are not listed on Form 990, Part VII.

Note. The sum of columns (B)(i)-(iii) must equal the applicable column (D) or column (E) amounts on Form 990, Part VII, line 1a.

(A) Name		(B) Breakdown of W-2 and/or 1099-MISC compensation			(C) Retirement and other deferred compensation	(D) Nontaxable benefits	(E) Total of columns (B)(i)-(D)	(F) Compensation reported in prior Form 990 or Form 990-EZ
		(i) Base compensation	(ii) Bonus & incentive compensation	(iii) Other reportable compensation				
MARY ELCANO	(i)	372,328	0	3,713	47,705	5,770	429,516	0
	(ii)	0	0	0	0	0	0	0
BRIAN RHOA	(i)	357,446	0	821	54,913	18,642	431,822	0
	(ii)	0	0	0	0	0	0	0
DALE BATEMAN	(i)	247,322	0	1,666	30,379	4,603	283,970	0
	(ii)	0	0	0	0	0	0	0
THERESA BISCHOFF	(i)	347,294	0	2,385	40,139	7,320	397,138	0
	(ii)	0	0	0	0	0	0	0
ELIZABETH O'NEILL	(i)	310,391	33,700	7,649	100,669	13,943	466,352	0
	(ii)	0	0	0	0	0	0	0
WILLIAM MOORE	(i)	348,020	0	844	34,160	18,648	401,672	0
	(ii)	0	0	0	0	0	0	0
CHRISTINA SAMSON	(i)	281,705	28,000	1,908	68,016	12,871	392,500	0
	(ii)	0	0	0	0	0	0	0
MELISSA HURST	(i)	309,423	0	425	38,623	13,337	361,808	0
	(ii)	0	0	0	0	0	0	0
JEFFREY TOWERS	(i)	357,710	0	1,296	11,642	18,669	389,317	0
	(ii)	0	0	0	0	0	0	0
JAMES HROUDA	(i)	433,414	0	81,257	71,135	10,503	596,309	0
	(ii)	0	0	0	0	0	0	0
GERALD DEFRANCISCO	(i)	318,031	0	2,376	18,001	3,926	342,334	0
	(ii)	0	0	0	0	0	0	0
SHAUN GILMORE	(i)	490,552	75,000	243,172	23,096	18,669	850,489	0
	(ii)	0	0	0	0	0	0	0
GREG BALLISH	(i)	335,202	0	1,271	34,270	18,648	389,391	0
	(ii)	0	0	0	0	0	0	0
RICHARD KANE	(i)	275,406	0	966	127,094	6,815	410,281	0
	(ii)	0	0	0	0	0	0	0
GAIL MCGOVERN	(i)	518,806	0	476,912	30,966	5,338	1,032,022	0
	(ii)	0	0	0	0	0	0	0

Under the preceding section "FDA fines the American Red Cross $47,778,000 for unsafe blood operations," it is unconscionable that Ms. McGovern received a $90,000 incentives/ bonus in 2012, while the Red Cross, <u>under her responsibility as *Biomedical Quality Assurance*, received FDA fines in a total of $25,758,200 for 2010 and 2012</u>.

American Red Cross

Corporate Governance System

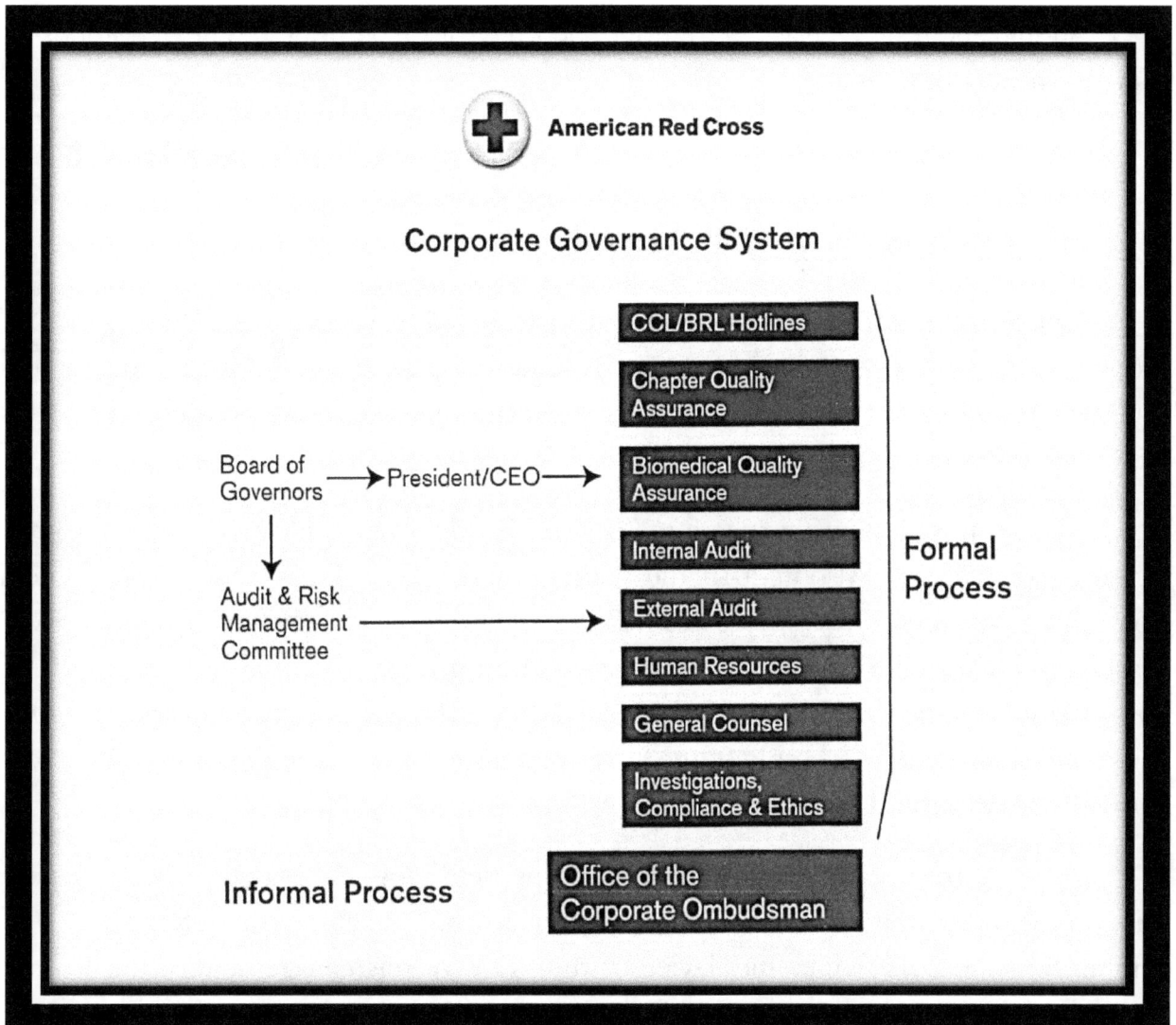

Source: American Red Cross 2012 Ombudsman Annual Report

Furthermore, examination of Exhibit VII (pages 86 to 87*)* and *Summary of Net Assets on page 88* shows how the Net Assets of the American Red Cross have gone down from $3,224,000,000 as at June 30, 2008 to $1,595,000,000 as at June 30, 2012. <u>Please note pension activity on this schedule, too.</u>

Further, Ms. McGovern was made aware by fax and certified mail, of <u>FDA Fines</u> to the American Red Cross – see page 28 of Adverse Determination Letter.

Based upon the above analysis, it is appropriate that the fate of Ms. McGovern's employment at the American Red Cross should be decided by you, the reader of this book!!!

Should she resign, be asked to resign, be fired, or be pardoned? The decision is yours to make, not mine.

LET'S MOVE ON>>>

2) *President of Biomedical Services*

Compensation for Mr. Gilmore is not surrounded by controversy, although it should be. Please refer to Exhibit I again. Mr. Gilmore base wages are set just under $500,000 in an apparent attempt to hedge against President Obama's possible $500,000 salary cap in the future.

Mr. Gilmore followed in the footsteps of Ms. McGovern, however, his sign-on incentive was $75,000. Also in 2010, the "Compensation and Management Development Committee" awarded Mr. Gilmore $240,627 "standard relocation Policy" for his move to Washington, D.C. (IRS Form 990). It is important to note that Mr. Gilmore received non-taxable benefits for $59,218 for the years 2010, 2011 and 2012 (averaging $19,740 per year) and is another example of the "Compensation Committee's" work – I do not know the answer to this situation.

It is most disturbing that the "Compensation and Management Development Committee" awarded Mr. Gilmore $69,657 in retirement deferred compensation in 2011, while fines <u>levied by the FDA for mismanagement of the Biomedical Services</u> (blood segment of the American Red Cross) amounted to a total of $6,390,000 in 2010 as previously stated.

Based upon the above analysis, it is appropriate that the fate of Mr. Gilmore's employment at the American Red Cross should be decided by you, the reader of this book!!!

Should he resign, be asked to resign, be fired, or be pardoned? The decision is yours to make, not mine.

LET'S MOVE ON>>>

3) *Executive VP, Biomedical Services*

Compensation for Mr. Hrouda is not surrounded by controversy, although it should be. Mr. Hrouda is the highest paid employee in the American Red Cross with an average annual compensation reported to the IRS of over $600,000 per year. Compensation in 2009 included a bonus/ incentive of $41,000 for relocation reimbursement. Mr. Hrouda's moving reimbursement is fractional of Ms. McGovern's ($613,527). Also, in the year 2009, "other taxable benefits" of $147,916 were not explained.

It is most disturbing that the "Compensation and Management Development Committee" awarded Mr. Hrouda "bonus/incentives" of $63,000 in 2011 and $76,755 in 2012 (totaling $139,755) while <u>fines levied by the FDA for mismanagement of the Biomedical Services</u> (blood segment of the American Red Cross) amounted to a total of $25,758,200 for years 2010 and 2012 – <u>what the HELL'S going on here</u>???

Further, Mr. Hrouda was also made aware by fax and certified mail, of <u>FDA Fines</u> to the American Red Cross – see pages 46-50 of Christopher's Book, for select pages of the Adverse Determination Letter.

Based upon the above analysis, it is appropriate that the fate of Mr. Hrouda's employment at the American Red Cross should be decided by you, the reader of this book!!!

Should he resign, be asked to resign, be fired, or be pardoned? The decision is yours to make, not mine.

LET'S MOVE ON>>>

4) *Division VP, Biomedical Services*

Ms. O'Neill's compensation for 2011 was omitted by the Red Cross. Her base salary averaged about $300,000 and she received bonus incentives of $33,700 and $16,000 for the years 2010 and 2012 respectively. <u>The bonus incentives were awarded in the same years the FDA levied fines of $25,758,200 at Biomedical Services for unsafe blood operations.</u> Please note, that Ms. O'Neill was also paid "retirement deferred-compensation" of $100,669 and $109,604 in 2009 and 2010, respectively.

Based upon the bonuses paid $49,700 during the years FDA fined the Red Cross and deferred compensation of $210,273 ($100,669 + $109,604) it is appropriate that the fate on Ms. O'Neil employment at the American Red Cross should be decided by you, the reader of this book!!!

Should she resign, be asked to resign, be fired, or be pardoned? The decision is yours to make, not mine.

LET'S MOVE ON>>>

5) *Division VP, Biomedical Services*

Mr. Brown's Total Compensation Reported to IRS in 2011 was $432,058. Please note he received a sign on bonus of $16,500, deferred compensation of $122,097 and non-taxable income $17,442. Although we do not know the fate of Mr. Brown in 2012, he was a member of the Biomedical Services "team."

Should he resign, be asked to resign, be fired, or be pardoned? The decision is yours to make, not mine.

LET'S MOVE ON>>>

6) *General Council Secretary*

Please refer to Exhibit II for Ms. Elcano's compensation profile – specifically, the year 2009.

It appears when Mark V. Everson was "asked" to leave the American Red Cross as "President & CEO" in late 2007, Ms. Elcano filled the position as interim President & CEO, until Ms. McGovern was hired in June 2008. Accordingly, Ms Elcano was awarded $110,000 in "bonus/ incentives" and $52,934 in "other taxable benefits. The monies were not paid until 2009.

Based upon the above analysis, it is appropriate that the fate of Ms. Elcano's employment at the American Red Cross should be decided by you, the reader of this book!!!

Further, Ms. Elcano was made aware by fax and certified mail, of <u>FDA Fines</u> to the American Red Cross – see page 28 of Adverse Determination Letter.

Should she resign, be asked to resign, be fired, or be pardoned? The decision is yours to make, not mine.

COMPENSATION SURVEYS

THE AMERICAN NATIONAL RED CROSS

FINANICAL SURVEY OF SELECT EMPLOYEES

Name	Position	Year		TOTAL COMPENSATION PERORTED TO IRS
Gail McGovern	President	2012	$	628,508
	CEO	2011	$	561,210
		2010	$	1,032,022
		2009	$	455,690
	(eight days pay)	2008	$	46,924
		TOTAL	$	2,724,354
James C. Hrouda	Exectutive VP,	2012	$	648,221
	Biomedical	2011	$	621,779
	Services	2010	$	596,309
		2009	$	642,286
		2008	$	524,664
		TOTAL	$	3,033,259
Shaun Gilmore	President	2012	$	543,660
	Biomedical	2011	$	573,933
	Services	2010	$	850,489
		2009	$	-
		2008	$	-

EXHIBIT I   **(Source: IRS Forms 990)**

base wages	bonus / incentives	other taxable benefits	retirement/ deferred-compensation	non-taxable benefits
$ 498,800	$ 90,000	$ 2,322	$ 29,243	$ 8,143
$ 498,800	$ -	$ 2,322	$ 54,750	$ 5,338
$ 518,806	$ -	$ 476,912	$ 30,966	$ 5,338
$ 220,000	$ 65,000	$ 161,867	$ 6,154	$ 2,669
$ 9,615	$ -	$ 37,309	$ -	-
$ 1,746,021	$ 155,000	$ 680,732	$ 121,113	$ 21,488
$ 421,610	$ 76,755	$ 59,436	$ 78,008	$ 12,412
$ 429,498	$ 63,000	$ 76,456	$ 42,587	$ 10,238
$ 433,414	$ -	$ 81,257	$ 71,135	$ 10,503
$ 377,313	$ 41,400	$ 147,916	$ 63,031	$ 12,626
$ 443,673	$ -	$ 48,689	$ 32,302	$ -
$ 2,105,508	$ 181,155	$ 413,754	$ 287,063	$ 45,779
$ 492,461	$ -	$ 1,539	$ 27,496	$ 22,164
$ 483,430	$ -	$ 2,443	$ 69,657	$ 18,403
$ 490,552	$ 75,000	$ 243,172	$ 23,096	$ 18,669

THE AMERICAN NATIONAL RED CROSS

FINANICAL SURVEY OF SELECT EMPLOYEES

Name	Position	Year	TOTAL COMPENSATION PERORTED TO IRS	
Mary Elcano	General Council/ Secretary	2012	$	424,756
		2011	$	459,452
		2010	$	429,516
		2009	$	550,189
		2008	$	495,187
Brian Rhoa	Chief Financial officer	2012	$	455,007
		2011	$	416,862
		2010	$	431,822
		2009	$	404,154
		2008	$	337,150
Dale Bateman	Chief Audit Executive	2012	$	292,548
		2011	$	316,572
		2010	$	283,970
		2009	$	290,960
		2008	$	242,034

EXHIBIT II   (Source: IRS Forms 990)

base wages	bonus / incentives	other taxable benefits	retirement/ deferred- compensation	non- taxable benefits
$ 370,922	$ -	$ 3,564	$ 43,899	$ 6,371
$ 369,183	$ -	$ 3,564	$ 81,199	$ 5,506
$ 372,328	$ -	$ 3,713	$ 47,705	$ 5,770
$ 317,946	$ 110,000	$ 52,934	$ 63,523	$ 5,786
$ 466,371	-	$ -	$ 25,816	$ 3,000
$ 367,055	$ -	$ 810	$ 66,383	$ 20,759
$ 354,598	$ -	$ 810	$ 43,051	$ 18,403
$ 357,446	$ -	$ 821	$ 54,913	$ 18,642
$ 271,208	$ 15,000	$ 39,983	$ 60,257	$ 17,706
$ 294,721	$ -	$ -	$ 39,429	$ 3,000
$ 246,325	$ -	$ 2,075	$ 39,774	$ 4,374
$ 245,188	$ -	$ 2,455	$ 64,575	$ 4,354
$ 247,322	$ -	$ 1,666	$ 30,379	$ 4,603
$ 249,740	$ -	$ 1,733	$ 34,813	$ 4,674
$ 232,615	$ -	$ -	$ 8,219	$ 1,200

THE AMERICAN NATIONAL RED CROSS

FINANICAL SURVEY OF SELECT EMPLOYEES

Name	Position	Year		TOTAL COMPENSATION PERORTED TO IRS
Mark Everson	President & CEO 29-May-07 Fired 27-Nov-07	2007	$	280,637
Elizabeth O'Neill	Division VP Biomedical Services	2012	$	382,787
		2011		
		2010	$	466,352
		2009	$	444,023
		2008	$	-
Mary-Alice Frank	CEO Greater Cleveland Area	2012	$	-
		2011	$	-
		2010	$	-
		2009	$	545,882
		2008	$	-

EXHIBIT III   **(Source: IRS Forms 990)**

base wages	bonus / incentives	other taxable benefits	retirement/ deferred- compensation	non- taxable benefits
$ 262,385	$ -	$ 1,250	$ 17,002	$ -
$ 309,109	$ 16,000	$ 2,080	$ 40,581	$ 15,017
$ 310,391	$ 33,700	$ 7,649	$ 100,669	$ 13,943
$ 289,911	$ -	$ 30,736	$ 109,604	$ 13,772
$ 221,364	$ 134,089	$ 19,752	$ 168,881	$ 1,796

THE AMERICAN NATIONAL RED CROSS,

FINANICAL SURVEY OF SELECT EMPLOYEES

Name	Position	Year	TOTAL COMPENSATION PERORTED TO IRS
Theresa Bischoff	CEO Greater New York	2012	$ -
		2011	$ -
		2010	$ -
		2009	$ 471,417
		2008	$ -
William Moore		2012	$ 397,816
		2011	Omitted
		2010	$ 401,672
		2009	$ 408,974
		2008	$ -
Jeffery Towers	Chief Development Officer	2012	$ -
		2011	$ -
		2010	$ 389,317
		2009	$ 309,481
		2008	$ -

EXHIBIT IV   **(Source: IRS Forms 990)**

base wages	bonus / incentives	other taxable benefits	retirement/ deferred- compensation	non- taxable benefits
346,054	$ 41,250	$ 17,664	$ 59,323	$ 7,126
346,107	$.	$ 810	$ 30,588	$ 20,341
348,020	$.	$ 844	$ 34,160	$ 18,648
312,224	$ 24,058	$ 16,653	$ 39,239	$ 16,800
357,710	$.	$ 1,296	$ 11,642	$ 18,669
212,179	$ 52,500	$ 32,448	$ 1,625	$ 10,729

THE AMERICAN NATIONAL RED CROSS

FINANICAL SURVEY OF SELECT EMPLOYEES

Name	Position	Year	TOTAL COMPENSATION PERORTED TO IRS
Christina Samson	Chief	2012	$ 369,303
	Investment	2011	$ 404,891
	Officer	2010	$ -
		2009	$ -
		2008	$ -
Gerald Defrancisco	President	2012	$ 413,522
	Humanitarian	2011	$ 452,194
	Services	2010	$ -
		2009	$ -
		2008	$ -
Kathryn Waldman	VP	2012	$ 394,309
	Quality Control	2011	$ 432,622
		2010	$ -
		2009	$ -
		2008	$ -

EXHIBIT V   (Source: IRS Forms 990)

base wages	bonus / incentives	other taxable benefits	retirement/ deferred- compensation	non- taxable benefits
$ 275,571	$ 25,910	$ 2,938	$ 51,188	$ 13,696
$ 279,594	$ 40,618	$ 2,938	$ 68,850	$ 12,891
$ 362,800	$ -	$ 3,564	$ 41,115	$ 6,043
$ 359,300	$ -	$ 3,168	$ 84,500	$ 5,226
$ 275,806	$ 48,795	$ 1,574	$ 58,762	$ 9,372
$ 245,173	$ 47,220	$ 1,574	$ 129,764	$ 8,891

THE AMERICAN NATIONAL RED CROSS

FINANICAL SURVEY OF SELECT EMPLOYEES

Name	Position	Year	TOTAL COMPENSATION PERORTED TO IRS
Greg Ballish	CRM Director	2011	$ 460,565
Joseph Becker	VP Atlantic Coast Division	2011	$ 462,106
Stephen Brown	Div. VP Bio Services	2011	$ 431,058
Joan Manning	VP	2011	$ 449,566
Suzanne DeFrancis	Chief, Public Affairs	2012	$ 380,144
Melissa Hurst	SVP Human Resources	2012	$ 371,434
Neal Litvack	Chief Development Officer	2012	$ 353,122

EXHIBIT VI   **(Source: IRS Forms 990)**

base wages	bonus / incentives	other taxable benefits	retirement/ deferred-compensation	non-taxable benefits
$ 332,914	$ 60,750	$ 1,242	$ 47,258	$ 18,401
$ 260,348	$ -	$ 117,789	$ 66,363	$ 17,606
$ 271,773	$ 16,500	$ 3,246	$ 122,097	$ 17,442
$ 276,927	$ 28,500	$ 1,989	$ 124,380	$ 17,770
$ 325,748	$ -	$ 3,382	$ 35,735	$ 15,279
$ 318,879	$ -	$ 493	$ 37,784	$ 14,268
$ 310,323	$ -	$ 1,677	$ 22,080	$ 19,042

BOARD OF GOVERNORS

The Board of Governors has various committees that provide information to aid in the decision making process.

It is imperative to note that the number of Governors has decreased from 48 in 2006 to 20 in 2012 and estimated hours per week spent on Red Cross work from 8 to 4, accordingly (IRS Forms 990). As a result, the decrease in the number of Governors has not increased the number of hours a Governor devotes to the Corporation. Has the reduction in Governors hours (on average) made the Board more efficient, or has it shifted previously Board members' work to American Red Cross employees? If American Red Cross employees are performing Governor's duties, the <u>independence</u> that should exist between the Governors and employees is <u>seriously impaired</u>. The merging or dissolving of committees has, in all likelihood, occurred within the Corporation.

The "Compensation and Management Development Committee" has been addressed at various times in this chapter because of the information provided on the committee's activities are widely disclosed in the IRS tax forms 990. The information from the tax return provides a <u>reflection</u> on the activities of the Board of Governors. I have previously indicated how the "Compensation Committee" seemingly makes arbitrary decisions based on "guidelines" that are not available outside the Corporation. It appears the "Compensation Committee" draws up contracts and extends "standard" contracts to new and existing employees at will. Sign on incentives are also seemingly awarded at the will of the "Compensation Committee." The Fact that there is a contract with an executive employee does not necessarily mean the proposed compensation is consistently stated or represented as wages. Please take note from select executive compensations how the <u>categories vary</u>, as noted in Exhibits I to VI and shown, in part, on page 75.

	O'Neill 2010	Becker 2011	Ballish 2011	Rhoa 2012
Base Wages	$310,391	$260,348	$332,914	$367,055
Bonus/Incentives	$33,700	-	$60,750	-
Other Taxable Benefits	$7,649	$117,789	$1,242	$810
Retirement/Deferred-Comp.	$100,669	$66,363	$47,258	$66,383
Non-Taxable Benefits	$13,943	$17,606	$18,401	$20,759
Total Compensation	**$466,352**	**$462,106**	**$460,565**	**$455,007**

	McGovern 2009	McGovern 2010	Gilmore 2010
Base Wages	$220,000	$518,806	$490,552
Bonus/Incentives	$65,000	-	$75,000
Other Taxable Benefits	$161,867	$476,912	$243,172
Retirement/Deferred-Comp.	$6,154	$30,966	$23,096
Non-Taxable Benefits	$2,669	$5,338	$18,669
Total Compensation	**$455,690**	**$1,032,022**	**$850,489**

(Source: IRS Forms 990)

PENSION PLAN

PREFACE

As a general comment, the pension plan is <u>not</u> conservative and is subject to large variations in market value of assets. Pension plan accounting is a specialty form of "accounting" and not easily understood. There have been many gyrations in the American Red Cross's pension plan since 2006 and they are beyond the scope of this presentation, except, for the three notations (Part A, B, C) I have presented below:

PART A
PENSION FUND ACTIVITY:

2008	($77,000,000)
2009	($408,000,000)
2010	($86,000,000)
2011	$9,000,000
2012	<u>($386,000,000)</u>
TOTAL LOSSES	**($948,000,000)**

The current pension plan assets are highly leveraged (Risk Oriented). I propose that the plan become extremely conservative, stable and funded each year for the well-being of the American Red Cross employees. A well balanced portfolio of common and preferred stocks, U.S. government securities, Corporate bonds, money market funds, mutual funds, for example — certainly <u>not</u> hedge funds, commodities, venture capital, derivatives, and the like. One of the most important responsibilities of pension plan management is to provide a stable plan that offers sound, balanced, and conservative investing that will afford employees a certain security that their pension plan investments are in the best interests of the pension, with a high degree of certainty, over the long run. The pension plan must not be manipulated as a "scape-goat" by corporate financial executives and corresponding investment counselors.

PART B

CURRENT EVENT (12/31/12):

2012 "footnote 13"

"On July 12, 2012, the Board of Governors formally adopted a plan amendment to the Retirement System of the American National Red Cross, <u>freezing</u> benefit accruals as of December 31, 2012 for all plan participants, except for a small group of represented employees. This plan amendment will result in a curtailment gain estimated at $176 million in fiscal year 2013." (*Consolidated Financial Statements, 6/30/2012, p. 38*).

A "curtailment gain" means that the American Red Cross will not have to pay or vest $176,000,000 cash into the retirement fund each year. The plan vesting has stopped, <u>except for select executive management</u>. Such action may be devastating to employees who planned to retire, in part, with sufficient periodic pension benefits.

<u>Freezing</u> the Pension plan has a strong demoralizing effect on employees. Such actions <u>do not</u> aid in promoting a "<u>prestigious and satisfying</u> position one could attain in life!!"

PART C
DERIVATIVES

FOR

THE

PENSION PLAN ??

WHAT THE HECK IS GOING ON!?!

Derivatives investing is a sophisticated form of gambling, at best. To engage pension funding into a highly leveraged situation is, for the most part, reckless investing. The derivatives market has yet to collapse, yet to destroy investment portfolios and ruin the hopes of a pension plan; but, derivatives could very well do so.

"The value of derivatives has grown, while they remain very risky with the potential for large, unpredictable losses" *(TIME MAGAZINE)*. TIME also reports that there is a key problem with derivative investing –– "counterparty risk." Simply stated, "If you buy stock for cash, you cannot lose more than you invest. But if you sell $1,000 of derivatives and collateralize it by purchasing $900 of another offsetting derivative, how much are you really at risk? In theory, you can only lose $100. But if the person whom you purchased the $900 derivatives ends up defaulting, then you are on the hook for all $1,000 you sold. So you are at risk for $100 or $1,000? It's hard to know. Regulators try to assign weights and probabilities to determine capital requirements. But the bottom line is simple: if the whole market comes apart, everyone is at risk for a lot more than they expect." *(TIME MAGAZINE)*.

As you may have gathered from the example given, derivatives are complicated and implicitly risky. As the market stands now, let's all "jump on the gravy train" and proceed to the nearest casino and put everything on "Red" and spin the roulette wheel with our pension plan at risk. A detailed analysis of derivatives is beyond the scope of this book, although the saying "buyer beware" is appropriate. In addition, the day may come when we look back and say, why was our future livelihood entrusted to a few financial officers who led us down the road of reckless investing? There is nothing wrong with hard work, sensible pension investing and a prosperous retirement.

CAN ANYONE EXPLAIN THIS???

SOURCE-- CONSOLIDATED FINANCIAL STATEMENTS: YEAR-END JUNE 30, 2012

DERIVATIVE FINANCIAL INTRUMENTS

"The organization makes limited use of derivative financial instruments in order to mitigate certain risks. Derivative financial instruments are recorded at fair value." FOOTNOTE 1, Page 6

BENEFITS PLANS

FINANCIAL STATEMENT FOOTNOTE (10), PAGE 35.

"The following table lists the notional/contractual amount of derivatives by contract type included in pension plan assets at June 30, 2011 and 2012"---

Derivatives Type	June 30, 2011	June 30, 2012
Interest Rate Contracts	$75,000,000	$1,600,000,000
Commodity Contracts	8,000,000	52,000,000
Equity Contracts	16,000,000	190,000,000
Tail Risk Contracts	320,000,000	374,950,000

TOTAL	$419,000,000	$2,216,950,000

Percentage Increase: 429%

THE OFFICE
OF
AUDIT GENERAL

The "Office of the Audit General" (OAG) is organizationally under the Department of the Army. The OAG's auditors, in regard to the American Red Cross, must review and issue an independent audit opinion on the fiscal year–end (June 30th) audit work and verification of the audited consolidated financial statements by the independent certified public accountant (the CPA firm of KPMG, LLC in 2012). Simply stated, the OAG audits the audit performed by independent CPA firm of KPMG, LLC.

As a result of the limited audit procedures by the OAG, and reliance on KPMG's audit work, the "audit" of the American Red Cross's financial statements by OAG is a cursory one, at best. The OAG should not, in my opinion, be conducting an "audit" and rendering an accounting opinion on the financial statements with such a limited scope. The implication is that the OAG's resources are not being productively utilized. This is true. A more effective utilization of talent would be to have OAG conduct a <u>yearly independent evaluation of management's priorities and anticipated benefits</u> (IEMPAB) for the fiscal year's ending June 30th.

Sources of information to evaluate managements priorities could be, in part: Board of Governors meetings minutes; "Conflict of Interest Disclosure Questionnaire"; "Board and Committee Assessment Questionnaires"; "Individual Board Member Annual Self-Assessment" reports; interviewing Management (e.g., Chairman of the Board, Governors, President & CEO, VPs, managers, employees and volunteers as needed); attendance at applicable Congressional meetings; presentations by the Ombudsman – written and oral; current and previous financial reporting, operating budgets; press releases, business plan, clipping services: marketing and financial strategies; consultant reports; Statement of Net Assets (equity); Global disbursements of financial funds; relief strategies and reporting policies; blood management –– operational and financial, etc.

The "Board and Committee Assessment" questionnaire, as previously cited by title, is also an important document to analyze in evaluating management's priorities. The nine page questionnaire, for each director, intent is to "gather feedback on the overall performance of the Board of Governors of the American Red Cross and Board Committees." Some of the questions address the policies and effectiveness of the Board;

however, while the questionnaire is helpful, it does not necessarily address ideas flourishing within the Board. For example, an agenda for a particular Board meeting would normally be prepared by the Chairman of the Board's office. Perhaps, each Board member should submit <u>their own</u> version of the agenda, prior to the actual meeting (two weeks?), and all the proposed agenda's <u>(ideas)</u> would be considered in preparing the final agenda for the Board meeting.

Equally important sources of management's priorities are, what appears to be, "limitless" committees, some of which are a division of the Board of Governor's. The "standing" committees may provide information that is relevant to an IMPAB report. An applicable example would be executive compensation, as directed by the "Compensation and Management Development Committee."

Anticipated benefits would rely predominately on interviews (direct & indirect) with appropriate individuals as knowledgeable and experienced as possible. In many cases, the anticipated benefits would be the interpretation of various individual opinions, the facts at hand and objective presentations by the Office of the Audit General. On certain occasions the OAG may have to travel, make personal assessments, and perform hand-on evaluations of proposed benefits.

<u>While many concepts, sources of proposed finding, and presentation of various methodologies were presented, the most paramount consideration is the selection of what issue(s) that are to be addressed in the OAG's annual IMPAB report.</u> Although there may be recommendations from many sources, the final decision of priorities to be addressed, will lie within the OAG's Office. A relevant area of concern may also be the ARCH SYSTEM proposed by Bio Medical Services, which was previously discussed. Personnel with skills commensurate to the project will be assigned. If necessary, a respective outside specialist may temporarily be assigned to aid in areas of special expertise.

The findings of the OAG yearly review would be documented in a written report. The IMPAB report, along with the certified consolidated financial statements of the American Red Cross, would be presented to Red Cross's management and the respective Congressional sub-committee. Think of the incremental benefits the IMPAB report would provide management and the sub-committee, rather than doing a cursory audit by OAG. The financial audit of the American Red Cross would "rest" with the CPAs. Replacement of the OAG's "audit" with the yearly IMPAB report would require an amendment to the American Red Cross' charter.

It must also be noted that "management consultants" are hired by the American Red Cross and would not have the discretionary independence and the yearly reporting responsibilities as set forth in the above analysis. Consultants are usually directed to a specific facet of the business, a specific period of time (not ongoing) and specific professions. The audit firm of KPMG, LLC is not permitted to be a "management consultant" because there must be independence between the CPA auditor and the client, as promulgated by the American Institute of CPAs.

FINANCIAL STATEMENT
2012 FOOTNOTE "12"

Please note that I addressed the FDA fines and penalties in several previous segments of this chapter; however, I reserved this segment to analyze the relationship of the KPMG, LLC auditors to the American Red Cross. It is important to note that "footnotes" are used to explain important topics required by the financial community in relation to explaining an organization's financial statements. The most critical footnote in the 2012 financial statement is, in my opinion, footnote 12.

When the audit firm KPMG, LLC consented to accept footnote 12 as written, the footnote had no mention of any monetary fine amount. By not disclosing the monetary value of fines, the reader of footnote 12 does not get a monetary perspective of the fines and to be alert that Biomedical Services is in serious violation of FDA regulations. The footnote also states that an accrual (estimate of the fines) has been reflected in the financial statements without a given amount. One of the underlying principles of financial reporting is a term full disclosure of relevant situations. Also, while the amount of the FDA fine ($9,592,200 in 2012) is small in relationship to total expenditures, the 2012 fine is extremely serious. It is, in my opinion, an indication of possible incurrence of human sickness, and even death due to unwholesome blood collected, stored, and distributed to recipients by Biomedical Services.

Saying no more, kindly read the actual "footnote 12" as quoted from the American Red Cross's Consolidated Financial Statements. --2012, page 38:

"**Consent Decree:** In April 2003, The American National Red Cross signed an amended consent decree (the Decree) with the United States Food and Drug Administration (FDA) affecting Biomedical Services and its blood services regional operations. The Decree requires compliance with specific standards on how the Organization will manage and monitor its Biomedical Services' operations and formalized management of compliance related issues and provides timelines for their resolution. The Decree subjects the Organization to potential monetary penalties if it fails to meet the compliance standards. The compliance penalty provisions cover two general areas: (1) penalties for violations of the Decree, including violation of the Food Drug and Cosmetic Act and FDA regulations; and (2) penalties for the release of unsuitable blood products. Potential penalty amounts are limited to one percent of gross annual revenues generated by

83

Biomedical Services for products and services in the first year (April 15, 2003 through April 14, 2004) of the Decree. The limit is increased to two percent in the second year, three percent in the third year, and four percent starting in the fourth year and annually thereafter. It is the opinion of management that the financial statements reflect adequate accrual for potential penalties resulting from noncompliance with the requirements of the Decree."

While we see that the monetary amounts of the fines are $9,592,200 in 2012 and are not disclosed in footnote 12. Failure to do so draws away the attention of the reader from the reckless management's responsibility for the FDA fines.

KPMG, LLC AUDITORS

At one point, the Audit and Risk Management Committee, of the Board of Governors, stated "The Committee shall have sole authority in its discretion to approve all audit engagement fees and terms and to terminate the independent auditor." Further, the committee's regulations were stated to "Ensure the lead audit partners assigned by the independent auditors to the corporation (the American Red Cross), as well as the audit partner reviewing the Corporation's audit, shall be changed at least every five years." The tax partner, for example, has signed the corporate tax returns for at least the last seven years.

Keeping the same audit firm, for extended periods of time, can lead to complacency and possible stagnation in the audit approach and execution. It is apparent that a new large international Certified Public Accounting firm would be most advantageous. The need for a fresh look at internal controls, for one, is in dire need of implementation. With the proposed separation of the Office of Audit General (Department of Army) from the yearly audit function, a new CPA audit firm would assume full responsibility and accountability for the entire yearly audit of the American Red Cross. At times, the first year audit fee may be somewhat larger due to rejuvenated evaluation of internal controls and a more encompassing accounting, financial, and system recommendations by the new CPA firm. Rest assured, there is a new breed of CPA's highly trained in technology, domestic and international accounting, and auditing. Subservience and compliancy to management by an audit firm (for example, "Footnote 12") is never a healthy audit approach to financial reporting, in my opinion.

The American Red Cross

Statement of Net Assets (Equity):

Net assets are:

Total Assets

Less Total Liabilities

The term "Net Assets" has many synonyms: Net Worth; Capital; Shareholder's Equity (Corporation), for example. Statement of Net Assets, as used in this Chapter, is an accounting "tool" to describe the yearly changes in the components of Net Assets (Equity). The most important aspect of the Statement is that total Net Assets declined over 1 ½ billion dollars in a six year period. This statement is easily adaptive to a statement presented to the Board of Governors of a non-profit organization. The statement gives the reader a summary of changes and where certain favorable and unfavorable trends have occurred. (See chart on the following pages 86-87)

THE AMERICAN RED CROSS

STATEMENT OF NET ASSETS (EQUITY):

($ in billions and millions)

	2008	2009
Net Assets -- beginning of year(July 1,)	$ 3,224	$ 2,559
Operating Incme (Loss):		
Operating Revenue	$ 3,184	$ 3,302
Operating Expense	3,664	3,422
Net Operating Income (loss)	(480)	(120)
Pension Expenditure	(77)	(408)
Net non- operating investments gain (loss)	(108)	(359)
Net Increase (decrease) in Net Assets	(665)	(887)
Net Assets -- ending of year(June 31,)	$ 2,559	$ 1,672

(Source of data: IRS Forms 990)

EXHIBIT VII

	2010	2011	2012
	$ 1,672	$ 1,959	$ 2,192
	$ 3,588	$ 3,453	$ 3,155
	3,354	3,422	3,329
	234	31	$ (174)
	$ (86)	9	(386)
	139	193	(37)
	287	233	(597)
	$ 1,959	$ 2,192	$ 1,595

Summary of Net Assets
2008 through 2012
Presented below:

($ in Millions)

Beginning Balance of Net Assets as at July 1, 2008		**$3,224**
Operating Income (2008 – 2012)	**$16,682**	
Operating Expense (2008 – 2012)	**(17,191)**	
Net Operating (Loss)	**(509)**	
Non-operating Investment Losses (2008 – 2012)	**(172)**	
Pension Activity (2008 – 2012)	**(948)**	
Net Activity (Loss)		**(1,629)**
Ending balance of Net Assets as at June 30, 2012		**$1,595**

OBAMA'S BAND-AID

NO ONE AT THE AMERICAN RED CROSS IS GOING TO BE COMPENSATED MORE THAN THE PRESIDENT OF THE UNITED STATES, SO BE IT.

Currently the president of the United States earns $400,000, of which he forgoes $20,000 to show his concern for the hard times at hand. The new Chairman of the American Red Cross's Board (now a full time, paid position) salary will be set at $400,000. The new President (second in authority) salary will be set at $375,000. The next level of compensation will max at $350,000. It is believed an excellent life style can be maintained at these compensation levels. If, by chance, the compensation level for an individual is unacceptable, they are free to leave employment at the American Red Cross. The new Chairman wants employees who want to work hard, for self-fulfillment and to ultimately help others by helping oneself, too. Due to the fact management has performed without credibility, for so many years, the new Chairman and new President must work together to determine employment of management and their respective compensation levels, throughout the organization.

A final, but serious, consideration is the technique of compensating employees and the disbandment of the current "Compensation Committee." Company policy may restrict all bonus' to an employee up to 2% of their IRS W-2's gross income, and be made payable to the American Red Cross' pension plan. Employees with or without a bonus may make a personal contribution up to ½% of their IRS W-2 earnings, which will be matched by the American Red Cross. Contributions based on the above formula will not be "frozen" as dictated by the former Board of Governors. A new employee will join the pension plan after their second anniversary.

Management compensation will not have any further "extras" besides the 2 and ½% rules. The Chairman must turn the "craps-shoot" pension, into a well-run conservative plan that future retirees can rely on.

FDA FINES CONCLUSION

The first issue relates to the fact that, almost universally, accountants will not disclose certain facts in relation to the financial statements because the issues are "immaterial" to the business taken as a whole. The Red Cross assets and yearly expenses are each over one billion dollars.

The international accounting firm of KPMG may well take the position that the dollar amount of the fine in 2012 ($9,592,200) is not significant enough to disclose even though "footnote 12" discusses the fines in a narrative form, without the corresponding definitive amount of the fine. In addition, "footnote 12" of the financial statements states "it is the opinion of management that the financial statements reflect adequate accrual [estimate] for potential penalties resulting from noncompliance with the requirements of the Decree."

How much is the accrual??? I did not find it anywhere in the financial statements or IRS Form 990!!! Was the accrual a $100 dollars? or the full amount of the fine reported by the FDA ($9,592,200 in 2012) – we just do not know, even though conservative accounting would recognize the latter amount!!! Perhaps, somewhere, the number can be traced back to the auditor's work papers; I sincerely doubt it!!!

Second, the fines should "red flag," not only the American Red Cross, but the public, in a noteworthy way, that serious violators exist in health and life issues with the Biomedical Services of the American Red Cross operations.

Third, as previously noted in my analysis of "footnote 12," lack of a monetary fine will not give the reader of the financial statements an indication of the amount of fines under question. Relevant disclosure would indicate fines from 2003 to 2012 are $47,778,000.

Fourth, I cite, in part, an article written by JoNel Aleccia, Senior writer, NBC news, titled "FDA fines Red Cross nearly $9.6 million for blood safety lapses."

> "The Red Cross has been operating under the terms of a consent decree first issued in 1993 and then amended in 2003 to allow the FDA to impose stiff fines for ongoing failure to meet regulations and laws governing quality and safety of the nation's blood supply. The problems detected then were

the same ones that have not, apparently, been addressed now: overworked staff, sloppy clinical practices and inadequate record-keeping.

Despite repeated stiff fines and even the informal threat of ***criminal penalties***, (emphasis added), from some FDA officials, the agency has not succeeded in improving its record, the latest sanctions demonstrate." (January 16, 2012; fine issue on January 13, 2012).

Fifth, would present and potential donors contribute hard earned money to a charity that management does not earnestly prevent unnecessary fines in the amount over $47,000,000; I sincerely doubt it!!!

Six, for completeness sake, let's repeat that under management of Ms. McGovern (President & CEO) she received a $90,000 bonus/incentive in 2012, while the Red Cross incurred FDA fines totaling $25,758,200 for the years 2010 and 2012.

Finally, it is my opinion, that both management and the audit firm of KPMG hid behind what accountants call "materiality" and "full disclosure" to cover-up the lack of "Biomedical Quality Assurance" by management (re: Corporate Governance System" diagram, page 57).

FINAL CONCLUSIONS

Based upon my extensive reading and materials presented in this chapter, I find the American Red Cross issues – moral, social, management and economic – myopic and sickening.

I cannot emphasize enough the fines levied by the FDA. I know no one is perfect, and we accept that, but repeated fines, over many years, of the same nature, that could have been prevented, is immoral!!

The BioArch proposal is absurd. Fixing the current system, with new management, would make more sense. In my opinion, current technology is too risky for the management of a wireless system (complemented with lap-top computers) for processing blood amidst 40% of the American population.

I believe the cost of BioArch is prohibitive. The Board of Governors froze the pension plan contributions and then directed the funds toward financing the Bio-Arch System. Let's bail out of this "experiment" before it takes a serious toll on everyone involved. This may sound like a business policy decision, because that is exactly what it is!!!

The critical <u>social issue</u> confronting the well-being of the American Red Cross' employees is the Pension Fund. New admissions to the plan have been halted. <u>By freezing contributions to employees' pension funds and not management, subjects the present Board to discrimination action by employees vested in the American Red Cross Pension Plan. Hopefully, discrimination charges will, by itself, force existing Governors out of office and allow the corporation to be managed by only those capable and most willing to give their talent wholeheartedly to aiding individuals in most dire need of assistance — including Red Cross employees.</u>

I have consistently commented on the <u>management </u>of the American Red Cross throughout this chapter. Remember my "Financial Survey of Select Employees" (Exhibits I through VI)? I have purposely omitted Marsha Evans, a former President & CEO from the Exhibits, in order to specifically present the <u>"precedence"</u> set by the Board of Governors in the mid-2000s. One may ask, and rightfully so, why does this type of financial "management" exist at all. One may rightfully state, "Why is it so expensive to terminate an individual for <u>not</u> performing their God gifted talents to the best of their abilities?" Below are the facts I have extracted from IRS Forms 990, for former "President & CEO" of the American Red Cross Ms. Marsha Evans.

<u>Ms. Marsha Evans was terminated on December 12, 2005.</u>

Compensation (07/01/05 to 12/12/05)	$392,988
Severance pay (paid before 06/30/2006)	$247,500
Severance pay (paid after 06/30/2006)	$495,000
Employee Benefits ($25,681 + $4,536)	$30,217
Total Compensation after 07/01/05	$1,165,705

One of the most serious and recent <u>economic</u> problems the American Red Cross has addressed is compensation and employment of its workers. Under the leadership of Ms. McGovern, "President & CEO," she has terminated a significant amount of employees in an effort to save money and prevent a duplication of employee functions. While her efforts may have been successful, to an extent, the morale of remaining employees must be undisputedly low. It is tragic to note that many excellent employees in their fifties and early sixties have been replaced by individuals of lesser pay for the same responsibility; in other words, many employees were a victim of job promotions and salary inflation over extended periods of time, which ultimately caused their termination at a critical period in their lives.

I certainly hope the former employees who were terminated in the major cutbacks were afforded counseling to obtain new employment. The American Red Cross must start a personal approach to helping former employees. Periodic contact with former employees, perhaps by the Human Resources Department, would exemplify the humanistic attitude of the new Chairman of the Board.

It is also noteworthy that the <u>American Red Cross is not a viably run corporation</u>. Mismanagement is an accepted way of life. If things get "tough," the American Red Cross can always turn to Congress for appropriation "bail-out" money ($100,000,000) as it did in 2008. I believe the ties between the Board of Governors and Red Cross management is not independent, especially when it relates to the interaction of committees and employees of the Red Cross. The Board of Governors has many committees who cannot perform the duties required with only 20 members working on "average" of 3 hours a week.

I do not care to reiterate many of my findings previously stated in this chapter. I have, however, provided the reader with enough information to make their own decision on the credibility of present management to turn the American Red Cross into the "most prestigious and satisfying position one could attain in life."

If I were to rate existing management I would award it a "D" to "C-"at best.

Songs
of the Soul

"Americans"
Lyrics by Byron MacGregor, 1973

The United States dollar
Took another pounding
On German, French and
British exchanges this morning
Hitting the lowest point
Ever known in West Germany

It has declined there
By forty-one percent since 1971
And this Canadian thinks it's time
To speak up for the Americans
As the most generous and possibly
The least appreciated people
In all the Earth

As long as sixty years ago when
I first started to read newspapers
I read of floods on the
Yellow River and the Yangtze
Who rushed in with
Men and money to help
The Americans did

They have helped control floods
On the Nile, the Amazon
The Ganges and the Niger
Today the rich bottom land
Of the Mississippi is under water
And no foreign land has sent
A dollar to help

Germany, Japan and to a lesser extent
Britain and Italy were lifted out of
The debris of war by the Americans
Who poured billions of dollars
And forgave other billions in debt
None of those countries is today
Paying interest on it's

Remaining debts to the United States

When the franc was in danger
Of collapsing in 1956
It was the Americans
Who propped it up
And the reward was to be insulted
And swindled on the streets of Paris
I was there, I saw it

When distant cities are hit by earthquake
It is the United States that hurries in to help
Managua, Nicaragua is one of the most recent examples
So far this spring, fifty-nine American communities
Have been flattened by tornadoes, nobody has helped

The Marshall Plan, the Truman Policy
All pumped out billions upon billions
Of dollars into discouraged countries
Are writing about the decadent
War mongering Americans

I'd like to just see one of those countries
That is gloating over the erosion
Of the United States dollar
Build its own airplanes

Come on, let's hear it
Does any other country in the world have
A plane to equal the Boeing Jumbo jet
The Lockheed Tri-Star or the Douglas-10
If so, why don't they fly them
Why do all international lines
Except Russia, fly American planes

Why does no other land on Earth
Even consider putting a man or a woman on the moon
You talk about Japanese Technocracy
and you get radios
You talk about German Technocracy
And you get automobiles
You talk about American technocracy
And you will find men on the moon
Not once but several times

And safely home again

You talk about scandals and the Americans
Put theirs right in the store window
For everybody to look at
Even the draft dodgers
Are not pursued and hounded

They are here on our streets, most of them
Unless they are breaking Canadian laws
Are getting American dollars from
Ma and Pa at home to spend here

When the Americans get out
Of this bind, as they will
Who could blame them if they said
The hell with the rest of the world
Let someone else buy the Israel bonds

Let someone else build or repair foreign dams
Or design foreign buildings that
Won't shake apart in earthquakes
When the railways of
France, Germany and India
Were breaking down through age
It was the Americas who rebuilt them
When the Pennsylvania Railroad
And the New York Central went broke
Nobody loaned them an old caboose
Both are still broke

I can name you five thousand times
When the Americans raced to the help
Of other people in trouble
Can you name me even one time when
Someone else raced to the Americans in trouble
I don't think there was outside help
Even during the San Francisco earthquake

Our neighbors have faced it alone
And I'm one Canadian who's damned tired
Of hearing them kicked around

They will come out of this thing

With their flag high and when they do
They are entitled to thumb their nose
At the lands that are gloating
Over their present troubles
I hope Canada is not one of these
But there are many smug self-righteous Canadians

And finally, the American Red Cross
Was told at its forty-eighth
Annual meeting in New Orleans
That it was broke
This year's disasters have taken it all
And nobody but nobody has helped.
[Emphasis Added]

THE END

of

American Red Cross

Chapter

CHAPTER V

<u>A SOLDIER'S COMPANION</u>

OH I FOUND MY SOLDIER OF LIFE, STRICKEN WITH A BULLET TO THE HEART

YOUR LIFE IS IN DIRE NEED OF CARE – TO PATCH YOUR WOUNDS WITH LOVES BANDAGES.

AS WE SHARE OUR TIMES PAST, WE LOOK TO ONE ANOTHER WITH A PRAYER IN OUR HEARTS.

I SEE A WOUND READY TO KILL WHICH THE COURAGE OF A BATTALION COULDN'T CURTAIL.

THE REFLECTION IN OUR EYES GIVES A SPECIAL MESSAGE TO EACH.

WE LOOK TO THE LORD WITH THE HOPE OF REJUVENATING THE CELLS IN YOUR FRAIL BODY.

OH LOVED ONE, GIVE ME THE STRENGTH TO WATCH, LISTEN, AND FEEL WITH MY SOUL AS YOU LEAVE FROM THIS BLESSED WORLD.

OH LOVED ONE, YOU WILL LEAVE US SOON. PLEASE REMEMBER MY HAND HOLDING YOURS, MY TEARS ON YOUR CHEEK AND MY LOVE IN YOUR HEART.

IT'S TIME TO SAY GOODBYE, MY SOLDIER, REMEMBER ME AS YOUR FRIEND, YOUR CARETAKER, AND YOUR PARTNER IN THE ENJOYMENT OF LIFE.

GOODBYE MY SOLDIER, I WILL ALWAYS LOVE THEE IN SPIRIT.

GOODBYE MY SOLDIER…

GOODBYE…

CHAPTER VI

A FEEL FOR GETTYSBURG...

A SPECIAL LIFETIME

REENACTMENT!!!

The day was a special day…

It was Veterans Day…

I was holding my American flag on a five foot pole…

I had a firm grip on the pole…

I held the flag and the pole high into the air…

I was about to place the pole into the bracket attached to my porch…

Then!!!

I tripped and fell into the bushes…

The flag landed on me…

I was on the ground for four or five minutes…Got up on my feet slowly…

Raised the American flag high into the air once again…

Secured it into the bracket to wave all day…

I was wounded in the leg, even to today, a small price to pay…

CHAPTER VII

I

HAD

A

DREAM,

TOO!!!

BY

Christopher Paltz

MARTIN LUTHER KING, JR

A New Tribute

Operation LifeSaver

Songs of the Soul

"We Are the World
(USA for Africa)"
Lyrics by Michael Jackson, 1985

There comes a time when we heed a certain call
When the world must come together as one
There are people dying
And it's time to lend a hand to life
The greatest gift of all

We can't go on pretending day by day
That someone somewhere will soon make a change
We all are a part of God's great big family
And the truth, you know,
Love is all we need

[Chorus:]
We are the world, we are the children
We are the ones who make a brighter day
So let's start giving
There's a choice we're making
We're saving our own lives
It's true we'll make a better day
Just you and me

Send them your heart so they'll know that someone cares
And their lives will be stronger and free
As God has shown us by turning stone to bread
So we all must lend a helping hand

[Chorus:]

When you're down and out, there seems no hope at all
But if you just believe there's no way we can fall
Well…well…well
Let's realize that a change can only come
When we stand together as one

I just finished writing my chapter on the American Red Cross for my book and was exhausted, after spending about two months researching and writing the chapter. I went to my bedroom and flopped upon my bed and fell sound asleep.

In a matter of minutes, I was dreaming. The dream, as I remember, went something like this:

Geneva, Switzerland

I was leaving the World Bank Office in Geneva, when I ran into Bill and Melinda Gates. They were surprised to see me, being a world famous Certified Public Accountant that I am. After a short conversation, I offered them lunch, which they graciously accepted. I immediately stated I was making substantial progress on a book in aiding Africa by utilizing various concepts and approaches that were extremely innovative and attainable, too. As I mentioned some of my ideas, both Bill and Melinda were extremely interested in my concepts and optimism. The couple, in turn, discussed their experiences in traveling and aiding in disease treatment. Bill added that he and Melinda were going to donate a part of the Bill and Melinda Foundation to the African cause. I suggested we should formally combine our interests and form a new foundation in both our names. We were at an impasse as to what the foundation's name should be. So, we flipped a gold coin. I won, and the new foundation would be called the Paltz and Gates Foundation.

The Paltz and Gates Foundation
Washington, D.C.

When it was apparent the three of us were compatible to work together as a team, we gave ourselves the name "Musketeers" after "The Three Musketeers." After two weeks from our visit to Geneva, we were settled at the Foundation's headquarters in Washington, D.C. Selection of the city was due to the proximity to the White House, the Pentagon and the Capital of the United States. Upon the initial meetings in our new office we, the Musketeers, made several policy decisions. The first, and most important, was that all funds and efforts of the new foundation were to be directed to the overall benefit of the diseased and famished people of Africa. In addition, the plan adopted by the Musketeers would be called "Operation LifeSaver." We all agreed that a great deal of assertiveness will be required by each of us to be successful, in what we have to know, as our attainable "destiny" in life – beyond all prior successes.

The White House
Washington, D.C.

Bill and Melinda used their "names" (and mine, too) to gain a visit with President Obama. The Musketeers met with the President and Mrs. Obama in the Oval Office. Naturally the focus was initially with nicety talk as we quickly moved on to the subject of "Operation LifeSaver." I spoke first, since the endeavor was my overall plan. My presentation only lasted for about 15 minutes in general terms. I expressed the overall methodology of our proposed ideas and actions that may be utilized by the United States role in the plan. I stressed that the plan, while spearheaded by the United States, would also be supported by vast international resources too. Bill spoke next. He started by indicating the Paltz and Gates foundation was formed to join our individual talents in addressing a seemingly impossible task. Melinda then stated that I convinced Bill and herself that our efforts, in an <u>overall approach to Africa</u>, would make an untold humanitarian impact on life and freedom from want.

"Mr. President," Bill stated, "we will need time to evaluate military assets used, and proposed in our plan. The Musketeers must have a <u>hands-on approach in dealing with military ships and aviation planes to start</u>. We recommend that the Joint Chiefs of Staff be involved in helping us in our military proposals and opinions. The initial need for military commitments is that they can be relied upon more so, at least initially, then industry and personal gifts from the American and international communities. The Musketeers feel it is within our destiny to turn the African situation around in a most honorable manner. We are entering the last third of our lives with vast knowledge and experience that can be co-mingled to produce a bonding of talent that would otherwise never be possible or as productive as we perceive it. In an unusual respect, we, the Musketeers view ourselves as President Roosevelt, Admiral Nimitz and General Patton in our personal traits and abilities to get things done, with purpose, as during WWII."

The President was so moved by our overall plan, as it exists at the present time, he authorized the Musketeers to continue our vital work at the Paltz and Gates Foundation. President Obama stated that it was his desire to keep the plan confidential until we get full authorization by the African countries selected. President Obama said he would get the necessary feedback within two weeks.

Melinda also stated that the Musketeers would have regular communication with confidential contacts at the White House, who would, in turn, keep the President abreast of our endeavors. As the Musketeers were about to leave the Oval office, I stated speaking for the three of us, "I think granting leadership of the plan in our hands is a particularly wise decision for all parties concerned." A final comment by the President was he was going to have Homeland Security give the Foundation proper security and direct lines to the White House and the Pentagon.

The Paltz and Gates Foundation
Washington. D.C.

Bill assigned five analysts to gather as much relevant information as they could in the last week, in regard to aircraft carriers, amphibious assault ships, and aircraft. Upon returning from the White House, the Musketeers started reviewing the analysts' work. This process took four days to complete. When the review was completed I commented we were well briefed on the military status of ships and aircrafts in layman terms. Melinda brought up the question, "why are we reviewing the work of analysts when the Pentagon is to brief us on matters that concern us?"

Bill replied, "I found it is always prudent to get an independent viewpoint and also be knowledgeable when discussing important concepts and decisions. In other words, we have to be on top of our plan if it is going to be successful."

On Tuesday, the Musketeers finished their review of the analysts work by 4:00 p.m. Bill, "slouched" over in his chair, rose to his feet and stretched. At the same moment he said, "we are going to make humanitarian history as never known in the past. Our efforts will reach untold millions of people for decades to come. Bill then looked at the information assembled and stated we will also be "squeezing" assets from non-African nations that normally lie in the darkness of stagnation. I stated, "We will have to make personal visits to all non-commissioned ships that we will be considering in the plan." Melinda replied, "can't we rely on military reports to make decisions for us?" "No," I answered, "we must visit the actual ships to make sure we are receiving proper documentation and add any ideas we may have, too."

Next I stood and stated, "this is really more than we are attempting to do on the surface." Bill smiled and said, "the Musketeers and the Obamas are at parity now! This project is our life's mission and is greater than anything else we have accomplished to date. We will maneuver global countries peacefully to interact with one another as only war alliances have done in the past."

Pentagon
Washington, D.C.

The Musketeers arrived at the Pentagon and were greeted by Rear Admiral John McGregor of the North Atlantic fleet. Rear Admiral McGregor, after a short introduction about his military career, gave us a tour of the entire Pentagon. He stated he was surprised that non-commissioned individuals were able to tour the complex, even by orders of President Obama. The Musketeers assured Rear Admiral McGregor that everything witnessed today would never be utilized, except by ourselves, as a group of three. Besides our tour of the Pentagon, we stated we wanted to establish a rapport with our contacts and individuals we were going to be working with during the next several years. Bill stated "we were going to rely greatly on military information in the future, and would always require the best available data in the most expedient time framework." I added, "the three of us would be directing the use of many aircraft carriers, hospital ships, aviation aircraft, Amphibious Assault Ships and ground bases as we deem necessary." Rear Admiral McGregor immediately excused himself as a sweat broke out on his brow. In fifteen minutes, he returned with General Mark Skoler of the Air Force. Admiral McGregor stated we were correct in our statements of military authority, as ordered by President Obama. I was quick to reply we were instructed to work hand-in-hand with the military, keeping in mind that the President is Commander- in-Chief and has final authority in the entire operation. We were all reassured by the confidence instilled in us by the President's message to the group. Our professional relationships commenced as we began to discuss the Musketeers' initial plans.

One of the largest concerns of the Musketeers was the status of the USS Enterprise. I stated the ship, while not officially decommissioned, was being dismantled. I went on to say we have great expectations that she will be the flag ship of Operation LifeSaver. I said, "can we stop the dismantling process and get a study done on the whether the big "E" is capable of being converted into a *medical carrier?*"

"That order would have to come from the President, Mr. Paltz. I believe that communication must be made immediately," answered Admiral McGregor.

Within two hours the Musketeers and the Pentagon got the ok to stop the dismantlement and board the ship if deemed necessary by the Musketeers and Rear Admiral McGregor.

USS ENTERPRISE (CVN-65)

(NUCLEAR POWERED)

Operational prior to partial dismantling.

USS ENTERPRISE
Norfolk Naval Base
Norfolk, Virginia

Upon arrival to the naval base, Captain Douglas Smith greeted Rear Admiral McGregor and the Musketeers. Captain Smith immediately held a conference which included two ship architects, doctors and a helicopter specialist. As it turned out the Enterprise would cost less to convert to a hospital ship in its present state, because the work already completed would have been necessary in either case. The seven of us took a tour which I directed based upon my past audit experience and aided by Bill and Melinda. To everyone's surprise, Bill had to use the "head" because of his increasing irregularity – I personally think the excitement was too much for him to handle all at once. After a fifteen minute wait, we proceeded and took detailed notes and made directives to the military personnel for those items we felt were necessary. In turn, we were given many ideas that we would otherwise have missed.

After visiting the Commissary for some Navy souvenirs, we held a conference. All of us who attended were ready to work. Melinda was the first to speak. She stated that President Obama wants a cost estimate every two weeks. She also noted that she was glad that the ship was stripped of all her military weapons – this would reduce the conversion cost significantly. "Gentlemen, I think we are in far better shape in the conversion process than any of us expected. The Enterprise is basically in very good condition – the ship was overhauled within the last fifteen years at this naval base." I added that it is important to note that the whole process of dismantling her nuclear reactor would be eliminated for possibly another fifteen years. Admiral McGregor concurred that the reactor is in excellent condition and agreed to the fifteen year estimated useful life of the ship. Bill interjected that the computer system, while presently sufficient, would need upgrades for high volume of helicopter use. Easy access to the lower level (medical section) would be a prime issue and concern to all of us present. Naturally, Musketeers will have to work out the medical details shortly.

Surprisingly enough, Captain Smith stated he thought the whole project was farfetched. I immediately replied, "we don't give a damn what you think, and kindly dismiss yourself from this meeting." The meeting resumed immediately after Captain Smith's departure.

The meetings lasted for twelve days, while additional medical personnel were also brought into the planning process. Upon conclusion of the twelve days work, I stated to all present, that the reason we spent so much time working with the Enterprise is that it would decrease the "learning curve" when we address the other ships in our overall plan.

The Paltz and Gates Foundation
Washington, D.C.

Upon return to the Foundation, the Musketeers felt a great deal of accomplishment and, at the same time, an urgent need to continue the mission. Bill said, "can't we rely on military reports for the rest of the carriers?" I replied, "No! Look at all the substantial work we accomplished with the big "E". We must continue to afford the plan our fullest attention and continue our hands-on approach to guide us." "Sounds good to me Chris." "Me too," said Melinda. Since the carriers were "my" responsibility, I stated that there are six carriers presently in "moth balls." We must act quickly and make our evaluations as accurately as we did with the Enterprise. In addition, we will have the evaluations by ship architects, medical personnel and also the military view point, prior to our arrivals. We will be in the position to review their work and tour the ships in under two days each, based upon our experience gained with the Enterprise. Meanwhile, Homeland Security set up our security system and stationed two agents at both entrances to the building.

Next, we had a speaker conversation with President Obama while at the Foundation, before we were on the road again. Mr. President said he was pleased to hear about our endeavors and the positive outlook we had in regards to the Enterprise. We also alerted him to the fact we would be visiting five other carriers in "moth balls." He stated he was hoping we could finish our assessment of all the carriers within a month. Bill replied he will be moving on to "his" category – air craft – before a month's time. Melinda said that we were getting firm support from the Navy and the Pentagon. Many other subjects were discussed and the conversation ended by stating we will be at Philadelphia, PA and Bremerton, WA for the next ten days assessing mothball aircraft carriers and would give the President a synopsis of our findings upon our return.

USS FORRESTAL
Naval Inactive Ship Maintenance Facility (NISMF)
Philadelphia, PA

At 7:00 a.m. Rear Admiral McGregor and the Musketeers met with Air Force General Mark Scholer, and a committee of doctors, ship architects, helicopter specialists and a military minister. Each member in the committee gave a lecture in their respective area of expertise. General Scholar was asked by the Pentagon to attend the conference to ensure that the Air Force would be available if needed, by naval operations. The doctors present stated, based upon their personal experiences and analysis of square footage, the USS Forrestal should be able to accommodate the following medical needs:

6 Operating Rooms

14 ICU Beds

46 Wound Stations

1 Pharmacy

Medical Imaging (12 x-ray machines, two cat-scanners and a stress testing machine).

Functional Laboratory and Blood Bank supplied by the International Red Cross.

Imagine this, the ship can expand its medical compliment to

1,300 HOSPITAL BEDS

I looked amazed, and said out loud

DAMN WE HIT GOLD!!!

Rear Admiral McGregor, Bill and Melinda shared my sentiments, each with a gleam in their eyes!!!

The ship architects were next to make their presentations. Captain Charles Adams stated that the ship was sound and sea worthy. Volunteer architects were next to make their presentations. Volunteer architect Nancy Bowman also stated the smaller lift would be necessary in case of repairs to a given helicopter were needed. The fire extinguisher system may also need some repairs. Structural changes would be necessary but could be budgeted under $27,000,000. Priming and painting the ship white with large red crosses would cost about $6,700,000 each in incremental cost. Captain Adams also stated that it would be in the best interests structurally to have a sea trial before crossing the Atlantic.

Bill interrupted the conversation by stating, "Before we go any further, let's remember the date July 29, 1967 when the Forrestal was operating off the coast of Vietnam and a Zuni rocket was accidently fired from a F-4 Phantom Jet into a parked and armed A-4 Skyhawk. A bomb exploded causing a chain reaction of fuel and ordinance which also exploded and in doing so, sent fuel and flames to lower decks causing the death of 134 sailors and injuries to 64. We cannot forget this tragedy as it must never happen again, especially to a humanitarian hospital ship."

Helicopter specialist and veteran John Clever remarked that the deck would have to be sectioned off by painting designated areas for each helicopter, in a manner similar to that of the Amphibious Assault Ship USS Iwo Jima. A picture of the USS Iwo Jima was displayed on the wall. Obviously, transporting of patients from the helicopter to the medical evaluations unit requires the utmost skill and utilization of talented men and woman. I believe many retired veterans would be honored to serve their country again as patient transporters or serve on the USS Forrestal in any capacity they are able. Let's not also forget our WWII veterans, while in diminishing numbers, should be given the opportunity to serve again for the country they love so much.

Dr. Theodore Sperduto, a Presbyterian Minister, said he was ready to serve now, even during construction. He stated he remembers the holocaust when millions of Jewish heroes were killed – many by starvation and disease. "I assure you that the Musketeers at this conference will be dammed if they do not do what the creator refuses to do. American leadership rebuilt Germany and Japan while ignoring Africa – that was a mortal sin. It is also apparent in my mind when the Germans thought they were powerful with their machine guns. Oh, were they so wrong. It was the Jewish population in the camps who faced death with Bibles in their hands or, most importantly, in their minds. I further assure you that each persecuted Jewish individual sits at the right hand of God and every Nazi is cast to hell. I fully believe in Christianity, while I refuse to worship our creator, I preach only God will rectify the African situation by anointing a few with his graces. God bless the Musketeers for their presence on this planet as they will eventually die in pursuit of world rectification. I leave this world never to return, read your Bible, and get off your "butts" and work for the Africans in order to create a better world for all God's inhabitants." Dr. Sperduto then keeled over and passed away on to what he preached, as God wished of him.

Everyone was in a complete state of shock, not only from Dr. Sperduto's death, but his last sermon.

Within an hour everyone was back to work – there was no time to "wallow in the hollow."

USS Independence
USS Ranger
USS Kitty Hawk
USS Constellation
Naval Inactive Ship Maintenance Facility (NISMF)
Bremerton, Washington

Rear Admiral McGregor and the Musketeers arrived at Bremerton, WA. The tour was very similar to that of the Forrestal, except for the passing away of Dr. Ted. The ships evaluation teams met at exactly 7:00 a.m. The first priority discussed was the age of the ships. I asked if any of the ships would require a complete "overhaul." Admiral Stency replied that the USS Independence has been highly cannibalized and may not be a candidate.

"Let me ask you this, Mr. Paltz, are you considering re-commissioning all of the carriers?"

"Converting them is certainly better than building ships from scratch. One of our main objectives is to <u>utilize the ships we presently have and be able to convert them into humanitarian assets that will save lives.</u>"

Admiral Stency stated "I think you're wasting money with this whole project."

I said, "you are entitled to your opinion Admiral; however you are outranked by the authority specifically granted to us by the President. I believe you are out of order."

"Yes sir, Mr. Paltz," he replied. The eight days turned out to be particularly hectic with little rest or socializing. A positive note was the ships were disarmed and mothballing had no major impacts, except on the USS Independence. The other three ships required approximately two months work each before they could be re-commissioned. The carriers in contention would have approximately the same medical configuration as the USS Forrestal, according to the naval doctors at hand. The Musketeers each felt honored to be aboard the ships and looked forward to directing them in the years to follow.

The Paltz and Gates Foundation
Washington, D.C.

United States Navy Ship Presentation:

The Pentagon contacted us while we were at the NISMF Naval Base in Washington State, that the carriers Harry S. Truman, George Washington and John C. Stennis are candidates for "mothballing." I added that the major cost of operating the carriers is military, and once the ships are disarmed, the cost of operations would be a fraction of their current costs. That is fantastic news!!!

Melinda asked me how many aircraft carriers does the United States have commissioned? I replied <u>eleven</u>. "Oh yes, I remember that now. What about the Russians?" I replied one. ONE! … Yes one!

"While we are on the subject of aircraft carriers, Chris, how many are presently in operation in the world?" asked Melinda. I handed Melinda a sheet of paper which showed the following list of international carriers:

United States	11	Italy	2
Russia	1	China	1
Thailand	1	France	1
United Kingdom	1	Brazil	1
Spain	1	India	1

Bill also looked at the sheet of paper and commented that there certainly seems to be an imbalance here. The conversion of three American carriers into hospital ships would appear not to have a significant impact on our military position in the world. If we convert the three carriers, they could always be reinstated for military service, if need be. Melinda asked when was the last time these carriers were used in a military capacity, except by the United States? As far as I knew, not for a while. Perhaps a more interesting question is why do Spain and Italy need one or two respectively, for that matter?

While aircraft carriers, in terms of Operation LifeSaver, have been our initial objective, there are two other classes of American ships we need to address:

First, is the <u>Amphibious Assault Ships – LHA / LHD</u>. These ships resemble a small aircraft carrier, but are primarily used for helicopter assaults and troop transportation. Each ship can accommodate about fifteen helicopters on its deck at a particular point in time. In terms of helicopters we would like to utilize the Army CH-47 Chinook helicopter (the CH-47 can accommodate 24 patients on stretchers or 44 ambulatory patients) and the Navy C-53 Sea Stallion (the C-53 can accommodate 24 patients on stretchers or 38 ambulatory patients). Each "LHA or LHD" ship (presently 9 active in the United States Navy) can also transport about 1700+ marine troops aboard and disburse the troops from the hull of the ship by use of landing craft(s). In other words, <u>patients</u> could be transported to this class of ships by either air and/or by sea. Strategic use of one or more of the amphibious assault ships would have a most profound effect on Operation LifeSaver.

USS BATAAN (LHD-5)

AMPHIBIOUS ASSAULT SHIP

USS ESSEX (LHD-2)

AMPHIBIOUS ASSUALT SHIP

LANDING CRAFT

Photo Source: (1) File: USSEssexThailand.jpg. (2)www.AcclaimImages.com/_gallery/_image_pages/0420-0906-2513-4132.html

Second, are <u>Hospital Ships.</u> We have two commissioned hospital ships in the United States Navy. One is the <u>USNS Comfort</u> (T-AH-20) which is utilized in military wars and natural disasters. The USNS Comfort is stationed in Baltimore, Maryland and presently classified in a non-active "state of reduced operations." "Comfort" can be deployed within a five day notice and is considered more advanced than a field hospital but less capable than a traditional hospital on land in the United States. The ship has a total patient capacity of 1,000 beds with numerous wards and 12 operating rooms. The other United States hospital ship is the <u>USNS Mercy</u> (T-AH-19). The ship is stationed in San Diego, California and, like "Comfort," can be deployed within five days. Specifications of the USNS Mercy are almost identical to that of "Comfort." USNS Mercy is also non-active and classified in a "state of reduced operations."

Bill noted, that hospital ships sound ideal unless there is a military or natural disaster need. If that were the case, we would have to evacuate the ships – this condition would not be very practical. Unfortunately, we need a more stable arrangement, Chris. Sadly we will have to take the ships out of contention. "Wait!!" I said. "We could use commissioned amphibious assault ships (LHA/LHD), if properly equipped in advance, for <u>contingent</u> Humanitarian medical purposes as done in the past." "That is a good scenario Chris," Bill replied, "and it would directly free up 2,000 hospital ship beds for continued portal use in Africa."

USNS COMFORT (T-AH 20)

Photo Source: File:100128-N-5345W-292 The Military Sealift Command hospital ship USNS Comfort (T-AH 20) operates off the coast of Port au Prince, Haiti.jpg

"Melinda and Bill, I must continue in regards to military ships," I said. "By all means continue," said Melinda. "Well, there is good news and bad news. The good news is that the Navy decommissioned four LHA carrier ships. The bad news is that they sunk one and scrapped a second one. Hopefully, we will be privileged to have the USS Tarwa and USS Nassau (LHAs) joining the Operation LifeSaver's fleet." Melinda asked "Chris, how many proposed ships do we have in our scenario fleet thus far?" "As it stands now," I answered, "three active aircraft carriers, five decommissioned aircraft carriers, two hospital ships in a state of reduced operation, and two decommissioned amphibious assault ships giving us a grand total of… <u>12</u> proposed ships in our fleet." "Fantastic" was their reply.

"Finally," I continued, "there are many Navy and Army transport ships that should be available, in some reasonable numbers, to transport food and supplies along the central and western ports of Africa." Bill asked, while sitting in his Harvard smoking jacket, "Will we have to board all these ships, too?" "No," I said, "these ships are in excellent hands and quite able to function on their own. I have to leave now folks."

"Where are you going Chris?"

"I am spending time at the Smithsonian looking for ideas. I hate to break this to you, but I do have a life. I am taking my old girlfriend Linda there in my 1963 Corvette Stingray. I have to maintain my 'sporty image' you know."

"Chris do you want to borrow our limousine?"

"No thanks, we have the Corvette. By the way, our next mode of transportation is going to be a bicycle built-for-two."

"Ok Chris, we will pick you up at 6:30 a.m. en route to the White House."

"Fine with me. See you then."

At 6:30 a.m., the Gates limousine arrived at my town house. Upon entering it, I asked where's Bill? Melinda replied, "He is in McDonalds' men's room. He has been quite irregular since this whole project started." "What about the White House?" I asked. "The President is running a little late. Driver, please proceed to McDonalds to pick up Mr. Gates." Melinda said.

The White House
Washington, D.C.

<u>Summit One</u>

As we turned into the White House entrance in the Gates limousine, the three of us were totally surprised that the President, Mrs. Obama and the children were on the steps to greet us. We were elated by such an honor. After a cordial exchange of greetings, we entered the White House. Our conversation focused entirely on the children and their schooling, free time and how proud they must have been when their father was sworn in as President of the United States. Then, the President and the Musketeers immediately proceeded to a conference room and joined the Joint Chiefs of Staff.

I immediately gave my presentation on naval ships and my analysis of each ship – the presentation lasted uninterrupted for two hours. The President said he was very satisfied that my analysis was so comprehensive and accomplished in under a month. After a fifteen-minute break, we discussed military considerations again, which lasted for about an hour.

Bill, while feeling "snug" in his Harvard smoking jacket, said "<u>we are about to make the most serious decisions of our lives – which Africans are going to live or die!</u> We do not have nearly the resources to save everyone who needs our help at this point in time<u>. I believe we must focus on a few nations first and then expand our resources when available.</u>" The President, with a taut look on his face, said he was disturbed by the choices we would have to make. He continued, "Let's keep the situation foremost in our minds and have open conversations amongst us until that decision is made."

Operation LifeSaver will, within months, start the campaign utilizing United States Naval ships, aircraft, freighters <u>and</u> foreign assets. Bill stated we will have "his" respective analysis on aircraft within ten days. Melinda said her presentation, while involving mostly long term planning, would require immediate attention after Bill's presentation. <u>I stated that the tempo will have a sudden surge when progress begins to materialize.</u> "Hopefully when the plan becomes fully operational, in time, the United States and Russia will monitor Operation LifeSaver as a joint humanitarian team until self-sufficiency settles within each country," I said.

We must address another paramount issue – that is a "country negotiator." A "negotiator" will be the person assigned to meet with the President or Minister of a country and explain Operation LifeSaver to them. The initial need would be medicine, food, water, manpower and funds to administer the plan. A country's volunteer use of any acceptable hospital ship(s), cargo planes, helicopters, aircraft carriers, amphibious assault ships, and freighters in Operation LifeSaver would be representative of a country's leader and, in turn, of their countrymen's attitudes towards fellow mankind. Thus far Musketeers have assigned ourselves the following countries to negotiate with:

Chris: Russia, United Kingdom, Turkey and North Korea.

Bill: France, Switzerland, China, India, South Korea, Italy and Spain.

Melinda: Canada, Japan, Australia and the Philippines.

I made a proposal that we should attempt to have retired Admiral Mullen (twice Former Chairman of the Joint Chiefs of Staff) be a country "negotiator" because of his outstanding diplomatic skills. All present said "Aye!" I solemnly said, "it is clear in my mind when Admiral Mullen gave recognition to so many disabled veterans at his home, and as difficult it was to view the disabled gallant men and women veterans, he could not have been more honored by their presence. I believe a gathering is going to be a yearly tradition, at the home of each Chairman of the Joint Chiefs of Staff surrounding themselves by such honorable men and women whose bodies are permanently paralyzed, maimed and/or blinded." Admiral Mullen withheld tears. These veterans are as true Americans as you will find! Yet, he was happy to extend his military position to each veteran as a representative of their country.

"Chris, you mentioned at one point you have an estimate of the necessary funds per year to manage Operation LifeSaver."

"Yes I did Mr. President. I believe we can raise some of the funds by diverting the money you pledged for electric power – nine billion dollars – into Operation LifeSaver."

"Who else would help fund the project?"

"Most of the funds for Operation LifeSaver will be pledges from international government funds (estimated at four billion US dollars a year); the international commercial community (estimated at one billion US dollars a year); and one half a billion from United States private sector alone," I stated.

Bill, while brushing lint off his Harvard smoking jacket, said he expects the American commercial community to be extremely giving, similar to that of General Motors in WWII.

"Gentlemen," Melinda said, "the Musketeers and General Skoler will be visiting Davis-Monthan Air Force Base in Arizona tomorrow to determine which aircraft, if any, may be reinstated from our tremendous mothball storage facility. Chris will supervise the inventory observation while we keep an eye out for any suitable aircraft for flight missions in Africa."

Bill noted, to the members that as with the Navy, we are also trying to re-cycle aircrafts that are potentially viable, along with those currently used in the military, as much as possible.

The president concluded the summit by quoting hero Congressman Davey Crockett – "'Be always sure you are right – Then go ahead'… Let's continue to go ahead lady and gentlemen!!!"

Davis –Monthan
Air Force Base
Tucson, Arizona

General Skoler and the Musketeers spent the entire flight from Washington, D.C. to Tucson immerged in navigation reports and aircraft profiles. Bill and Melinda appeared somewhat annoyed at me for dragging them to this military air force base. Bill said "I hope this is not a wild goose chase!!"

"Relax, I am not a world famous Certified Public Accountant for nothing."

"Oh yah, we forgot – we are glad you reminded us of it."

I really could not get over the intensity on that airplane: it was like studying for college finals the entire flight. As the plane touched down, it was the alarm to pack up and get ready to depart. Just minutes before we set down, however, the Musketeers peered out the jet windows and were shocked at what seemed to be untold thousands of aircraft lined up in specified order, by type. Melinda commented, "I think I see what you are potentially talking about, Chris."

As we stepped off of Bill's jet, we had a reception party of a General and two Majors. After a few seconds the Musketeers realized they were saluting us too. In turn, we saluted them back.

After a quick snack, and a fifteen minute delay, because Bill was irregular again, we boarded a WWII jeep and started our tour. We were amazed at all the bombers, jet fighters and helicopters lying idle as we proceeded on our tour. I was happy to be the driver and maintain my "sporty image" with a general's helmet on. As we approached a group of aircraft, Melinda yelled, "STOP!!! Those planes are C-27J Spartans aren't they?"

General Skoler replied yes, with hesitation in his voice. "Those planes are brand new. What are they doing here?"

The General replied they were flown here directly from the assembly line. General Skoler continued by saying there are five more coming direct from assembly, too.

Bill stated with a stern look in his face, "we will take them all off your hands."

Melinda said, "Let's continue. I have seen enough here."

Fifteen minutes later, we looked at what appeared to be a hundred B-52s, some of which were practically disassembled.

B-52 STRATOFORTRESS

Bill immediately said "what series are those B-52's?"

"Those are mostly F and G series."

"Can they fly?"

"Yes Sir."

"Are they suited for dispensing medical supplies and food?"

"Yes, but they are expensive to run."

"We are talking about human life even though it may be costly."

"Yes Sir, Mr. Gates. We may have a problem with NATO and the Russians if we are to use them. That would require clearance and a special arrangement to utilize them in our plans." Let's move on. As we proceeded and were near another air strip Bill noticed another set of B-52s. I counted them and there were 37.

Bill said, "those B-52's are "H" series (most current) and should not be here! In addition, they are in violation of the SMART treaty [nuclear arms reduction treaty with the Russians].

General Skoler said they were "miss-counted" when the treaty was ratified. "Technically they are on loan to the Davis-Monthan Air Force Base, Mr. Gates."

The Musketeers took it upon themselves to tour the latest version of a B-52. I assured Bill and Melinda, there would be no way in hell I would have "missed" one third of the active B-52's current or reserved fleet – even if they were co-mingled!!

Next we focused on helicopters at the Air Base. I asked Bill and Melinda to keep an independent count as we went along. The count went along fine, as we noted there were what seemed countless helicopters that could be reactivated as, and if, a need arose. Almost all helicopters were stored without their propellers attached and sealed off from the elements. General Skoler stated that the rotors were also stored (in sealed wrappings). The Musketeers beamed as the plan was continuing as sought, in terms of potentially utilizing B-52 bombers, Chinook and Super Stallion Helicopters, if painted white with red cross's.

The trip turned out to be highly rewarding and advantageous to our plan.

The Gates', after a three- day rest at home, flew to Washington D.C. arriving at the Foundation by 11:00 a.m. I was asleep, in my dream, on the couch in my office with an aircraft report in my lap. After a few minutes of movement in the Gates' office, I awoke. The three of us had a short conversation on "Bill's" subject of aircraft and the impact on Operation LifeSaver. We all agreed that it is in the best interest of the plan that we be briefed further by the Pentagon in terms of aircraft utilization for rural and urban transportation of patients and supplies to medical carriers and land bases. The subject, while sounding easy, was far more complicated than we envisioned. Bill made a general statement that aircraft names become confusing and misleading when there are numerous series or versions of the same aircraft. Many times there are modernizations or upgrades and the name changes, too.

In addition, Bill chose to use the internet "Wikipedia Internet Encyclopedia" information because it is available to everyone and will not be classified information the Pentagon would prefer not to be circulated. I will present summaries of each aircraft because we are familiar with them and will only use them at <u>Summit Two</u> if asked upon. <u>Our education on these aircraft will be vital when we are actually commanding their use in Operation LifeSaver</u>. I will mention certain highlights when I feel it is appropriate. Bill said he had assembled many new ideas that he was going to present at Summit Two.

Helicopters

	Stretcher Patients	Ambulatory Patients	Number Made	Pay Load (pounds)	Run-way (feet)	Range (miles)	Cruise Speed	Country
ARMY CH-47F CHINOOKS	24	33-55	1,200E	7,000	vertical	750	193	USA
MARINE- NAVY CH-53E SUPER STALLION	24	55	411	30,000	vertical	621	173	USA
MARINE- V-22 OSPREY	-	24	160	14,360	vertical	1,011	277	USA
MIL MI-17	12	30	12,000E	7,961	vertical	308	155	Russia
MIL MI-26	60	80-150	316	40,000	vertical	1,213	183	Russia

HELICOPTER PROFILES

The <u>CH-47 Chinook</u> helicopter under consideration initially had three series of names (CH-47A, CH-47B, CH-47C) until 1982, when all CH-47s were upgraded to a single standard – CN-47D. More upgrades were made to the CH-47D and were technical in nature. The current versions are called CH-47F and MH-47G and were the result of the Army's "modernization program" (the updates included a mix of remanufactured and new aircraft). The new versions will ensure that this tandem rotor helicopter remains in the Army fleet <u>at least through the 2030s</u>. It is conceivable that the Chinooks will be Army Aviation assets for a century or more. In addition, Chinooks have served in the armed forces of more than 19 international countries and commercial service around the world.

The Chinook is currently used by the US Army, Army National Guard and the Army Reserve. The Chinook is going to be one of the major cornerstones of Operation LifeSaver because of the helicopter's ability to bring patients from inland on to the carriers for medical care. Finally, Bill stated, he expects initially about 250 Chinook helicopters to be active in Operation LifeSaver – extensively from the United States.

The <u>CH-53E Super Stallion</u> is the Marine's version of the Chinook. The CH-53A was originally a twin engine helicopter and delivered to the Marines in 1966. The first Super Stallion (CH-53E) was delivered in 1980 and included an additional third engine, a larger main rotor system with a seven blade, forward extendable in-flight refueling probe, and is able to host hose refueling from a surface ship while in the hover mode, etc. The USMC CH-53E is a <u>heavy-lift cargo helicopter</u> and, for example, was able to carry a disabled Chinook helicopter in eastern Afghanistan (2010) for a considerable distance. Presently, there are dozens of variations of the CH-53E.

The Super Stallion (CH-53E) could also be utilized to transport supplies from a freight ship directly to an Operation LifeSaver medical carrier and/or designated land base(s) without a ship actually "docking" into a port that may be over a week away from need. With the limited number of Super Stallions available, Bill estimates that only 40 would be available for Operation LifeSaver.

The <u>V-22 Osprey</u> is able to take off and land on aircraft carriers and assault ships horizontally and be stored in minimal space. The Osprey is noted for the engines being able to use a tilt-rotor engine for landing and flight. In addition, the aircraft has a greater maximum speed of all helicopters considered.

The Mil Mi-17 is designed for export from Russia. The Mi-17, a medium lift helicopter, has been purchased and used by numerous countries for both peace and war time missions. The United States is one such buyer of M-17s. In 2013, the United States formally acknowledged an agreement by the Pentagon (bypassing Congress), to purchase dozens of new and refurbished Mi-17s. The Pentagon stated that the Afghan forces had years of experience flying the M-17. The counter argument is that Afghan Air Forces could use American refurbished Chinooks that were about to be retired. However, the Pentagon stated refurbished Chinooks would cost about 40 percent more to overhaul and maintain than the M-17. The Chinook option never materialized. The Mi-17 purchase is only one example of the continuing financial commitment that the United States will extend to the Afghanistan government, even when U.S. troops are withdrawn. Bill estimated that while the United States is purchasing dozens of Mi-17s, the world community would contribute hundreds of Mi-17s to aide Operation LifeSaver.

The Mil Mi-26 is a Russian heavy transport helicopter. The Mi-26 remains the largest (physical) helicopter to ever have been produced in any number and still be active across the globe – placed in service during 1983. The statistics, as noted in my dream, are extremely noteworthy in every respect. The direct benefit is the aircraft's ability to carry 60 stretchers or, if need be, a maximum of 150 ambulatory (usually 80) patients. The Mi-26 has been utilized in many military/civilian humanitarian missions. For example, when an American MH-47E version of a Chinook was stranded in a remote area of Afghanistan, a civilian Mi-26 was leased to recover the disabled Chinook. The Mi-26 was able to transport the disabled Chinook (by hook) to Kabul, and later to Bagram Air Base, for a lease fee of $300,000. Six months later a second U.S. Army CH-47F, who made a "hard landing" 100 miles north of Bagram, was also recovered by a civilian Mi-26. Bill, with a annoyed look on his face, commented, "why weren't the Chinooks retrieved by Super Stallions who have a 30,000 pound lift capacity?" Neither Melinda nor I had an answer or a possible explanation.

On a positive note, I indicated it is noteworthy that the Mi-26MS is a full medical evacuation version. The Mi-26MS houses an operating room, pre-op section, laboratory, scrub facilities, and food storage. The Mi-25 has proven itself a capable performer in both military and civilian roles and has been part of NATO's humanitarian relief force when donated by a contributing nation. Bill estimated that possibly sixty five Mi-26s would be available, even part time, to transport patients and cargo.

U.S. ARMY CH-47 CHINOOK
(MEDIUM TRANSPORT HELICOPTER)

U.S. MARINE CH-53E SEA STALLION
(HEAVY TRANSPORT HELICOPTER)

U.S. V-22 OSPREY

(TILT ROTOR – HIGH SPEED – TRANSPORT AIRCRAFT)

Photo Source: File:US Navy 080708-N-4014G-063 A V-22 Osprey aircraft from the.jpg

MIL MI-26 "HALO" (~DOOMYCH / PD)

RUSSIAN MIL MI-26

(WORLDS LARGEST PRODUCTION HELECOPTER)

American Freight Planes, B-1B, B-52

	Status	Ambulatory Patients	Number Made	Pay Load (pounds)	Run-way (feet)	Range (miles)	Cruise Speed	Country
C-130 HERCULES	active	92	2,300+	45,000	3,586	2,360	336	USA
C-130J "SUPER" HERCULES	active	92	300	42,000	3,127	3,270	400	USA
C-5 GALAXY	active	270	131	270,000	8,400	2,760	579	USA
C-27J SPARTAN	NEW	60	21	25,353	1,115	1,050	362	USA
747-400F (BOEING)	active	fgt.	694	295,800	10,660	5,110	560	USA
747-8F (BOEING)	active	fgt.	67	295,800	11,000E	5,050	564	USA
C-17 GLOBEMASTER III	active	54	250	170,900	7,600	2,770	515	USA
B-1B LANCER "BONE"	active	bomber	100	125,000	11,000E	7,450	700	USA
B-52 STRATOFORTTRESS	active	bomber	744	303,000	11,000E	10,150	525	USA

FREIGHT PLANE PROFILES

The C-130 Hercules is a versatile cargo plane. The plane is able to dispense 42,000 pounds of air-drop cargo while being airborne or unloaded on land. Typical cargo could be food, medical supplies, water, passengers, trucks, utility helicopters, etc. – all of which is representative of Operation LifeSaver needs. In addition the C-130 is able to land on unprepared runways such as dirt "landing strips." The cargo aircraft is excellent for both rural and established settings – exactly in what we are in need of!!

The C-130J is an updated (state-of-the-art technology) aircraft that varies from the original C-130, while maintaining the basic advantages afforded to the initial C-130 users. I suspect our plan will be utilizing many C-130s initially because of the vast amount already in use and that the switch over to C-130Js will take years to complete.

The C-5 Galaxy is an excellent candidate for our cargo weight plan except only 131 were produced and carries no patients.

The C-27J is a new plane misconceived by the Pentagon and Air Force where technology surpassed the military usefulness before it was placed in operation. Bill said "we will not allow the planes to be used for 'training' while they can be used for humanitarian purposes -- I am sure the President will agree."

The Boeing 747-400F and 747-8F have basically the same operational statistics; however, the 747-400F has an inventory of 694 planes compared to 67 of the 747-8F. I believe the 747-400F will be our major commercial contributor, by sheer numbers alone.

The C-17 Globemaster III fits our needs, on average, with the other aircraft and will be a welcome addition to our fleet, although a relatively limited number were produced.

C-130 HERCULES

Photo Source: File:Lockheed C-130 Hercules.jpg

C-130 HERCULES

DISPENSING CARGO IN FLIGHT

Photo Source: File: US Navy 061210 –N-7770P-007 Bundles of shelters and mosquito nets are dropped from a U.S. Air Force C-130 cargo plane onto a field in rural Kenya.jpg

C-130 HERCULES

ALTERNATIVE CARGO DELIVERY

C-130 HERCULES

-FLAIRS-

AWESOME

AWESOME

AWESOME

747 BOEING

CARGO AIRCRAFT

This picture denotes standard size cargo pallets (freight containers) being loaded into the UPS freight aircraft (747-400F). Pallets are the same size, and are loaded when the front of the aircraft is in an upright position, as noted.

Photo Source: (UPS) "UPS Pilots, Cargo Carriers File Papers in Duty Rule Case" by Bill Carey

747 BOEING

IN FLIGHT

C-17 GLOBEMASTER III

RESCUE MISSION IN PROGRESS!!!

C-5M SUPER GALAXY

"The C-5 Galaxy is one the largest aircraft in the world and the largest airlifter in the U.S. Air Force Inventory. It can carry outsized cargo intercontinental ranges and can take off or land in relatively short distances. Ground crews can load and off load the C-5 simultaneously at the front and rear cargo openings since the nose and aft doors open the full width and height of the cargo compartment."-Wikimedia Commons Description

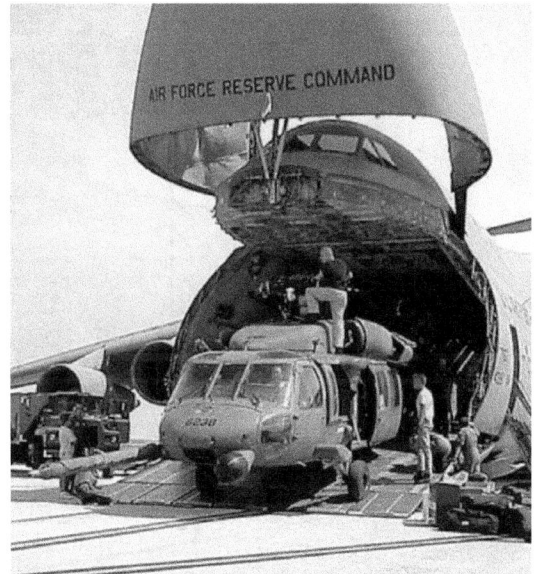

Photo Source: (1) File: Usaf.c5.galaxy.750pix.jpg (2) "Mighty Planes: C-5m Super Galaxy." 2013.03.11. http://www.macaucabletv.com/en/2013/post14130/mighty-planesc-5m-super-galaxy.html

Foreign Freight Planes & Tu-160

	Status	Ambulatory Patients	Number Made	Pay Load (pounds)	Run-way (feet)	Range (miles)	Cruise Speed	Country
ANTONOV AN-124	active	88-352	n/a	330,000	8,270	3,230	490	Russia
TRANSALL C-160	active	93	214	35,275	8,300	1,150	368	German/ French
SHAANIX Y-8	active	90	269	44,000	4,200	3,480	410	China
ILYUSHIN IL-76	active	140	960	92,594	5,580	2,670	472	Russian
TUPOLDEV TU-160	Active	bomber	36	363,750	11,000E	7,640	596	Russian

FOREIGN FREIGHT PLANE PROFILE

The Antonov An-124 is an extremely large Russian freight carrier. The payload is a remarkable 330,000 pounds and joins the ranks of American freighters: C-5 Galaxy, C-17, 747-400F, and the 747-8F. The runway footage is also shorter than the American counterparts. In addition, the aircraft can carry up to 352 ambulatory patients.

RUSSIAN ANTONOV AN-124

Bill did note that the An-124, C-5, 747-400F, 747-8F runway requirements may cause concern in respect to existing runways – many African runways will have to be lengthened to meet our proposed take-off requirements. The use of B-52s (to drop food, for example) would require a runway of over 1,200 feet. In due course, we will also have to determine the extensive building of dirt runways, of a high quality, in remote areas, too. The challenge in this area alone will require our immediate attention, once President Obama determines which countries are initially selected for Operation LifeSaver.

Over the last two weeks, the Foundation received hundreds of updates on the work status of our aircraft carriers. Each carrier was progressing along schedule, except the USS Independence, which is beyond reasonable repair.

Photo Source: (1) File:Russian heavylift freighter AN-124.jpg (2) http://en.wikipedia.org/wiki/Cargo_aircraft

I am supervising by a progress schedule called a "PERT" chart (Program Evaluation Review Technique) on each ship that shows "bottlenecks" in a projects progress, for one. PERT charts were used in WWII to determine which targets to bomb – in effect targeting critical industries that would cause "ripple" damage in Hitler's war machine. Today PERT is utilized by management to determine if a project is progressing as planned. The focus is on correcting miscalculations that may ultimately cause material delays in finishing a project in a timely manner.

The White House
Washington, D.C.
Summit Two

Bill was scheduled to speak first.

Before he presented his aircraft lecture, Bill made a notation, out of the "blue sky," of his concern for the millions of people starving in the African continent. At this point, Bill made note of my father's contribution to the war effort in WWII. Chris' father, Walter Paltz, a MIT-Chemical Engineer at ESSO, was one of a handful of scientists who discovered synthetic rubber from petroleum oil. Such a discovery was critical to the United States in WWII, when Burma's natural rubber was cut off by the Japanese. I was thankful for Bill's acknowledgment as he also stated it was <u>necessary</u> for that kind of talent at the present time, too.

Bill proposed that while he was the majority shareholder of Microsoft Corporation, he was going to develop a separate division for preservation/packaging of food for a period of, let's say, five to ten years without contamination and refrigeration, thereby <u>eliminating starvation in Africa!!!</u> The new Microsoft division would be spearheaded by the genius existing within the corpus of Microsoft and the most noted chemical engineers in the United States. Bill projected profits of billions of dollars per year, once the patents were secured. As a passing thought, he commented, "such a food packet (container) may be a petroleum byproduct or a combination thereof. I am insistent," Bill stated, "that all secured profits generated by **Division Two** of Microsoft be used for prioritized needs of Africa as decided by the Musketeers. Such a discovery, if properly managed, could eliminate starvation of untold numbers of people and eliminate the want of food from the African continent!!! President Obama stated that he was sure that if Bill Gates set his mind to something conceivable, the likelihood of success would be emanate, and, in this case, be a "pay-back" to society, the likes of which have yet to be seen!!!

Next Bill proceeded into his presentation of aircrafts, which was very similar to the one he made to Melinda and me at the Foundation. The videos and written information were well received by all attending – even by General Skoler (Air Force Chief of Staff). <u>Bill also stated that the extensive research about aircraft would be most helpful when the Musketeers are in the position to direct available aircraft on land and sea.</u> Bill entertained several questions all of which were related to aircraft and their role in aiding medical carriers and air lift transportation.

BILL`s C-130 CARGO PLANE PLAN:

In a U.S. domestic disaster, C130 planes would be used as a first response to devastated areas where human life is at risk. The C-130s are able to airlift and drop supplies (medical, food, water, for example), as well as manpower, while in flight. In addition, the C-130s can land at established airports, or remote dirt runways greater than 3,586 feet in length. Transporting patients from an emergency area to a hospital(s) near a landing ground is also a function of the C-130. (The aircraft is able to transport a mix of 24 stretchers or 92 ambulatory patients). Please bear in mind, the C-130s crews must be highly trained to co-ordinate their efforts in <u>conjunction</u> with both the American Red Cross and National Guards. Initial response time and subsequent airlifts, are critical in terms of saving and maintaining human life.

The United States has approximately 167 domestic C-130s -- excluding the Reserves and Air National Guard. Bill noted from actual photos that there is an <u>abundant capacity</u> at Scott Air Force Base (Illinois) to operate 75 C-130s. Scott AFB is centrally located in the United States. With full fuel, C-130s have a range to reach any point in the congruous state of the country in their initial flight. After unloading the first cargo, the C-130s would fly directly to the <u>closet secondary base</u> for cargo and fuel refills.

C–130 FORCES

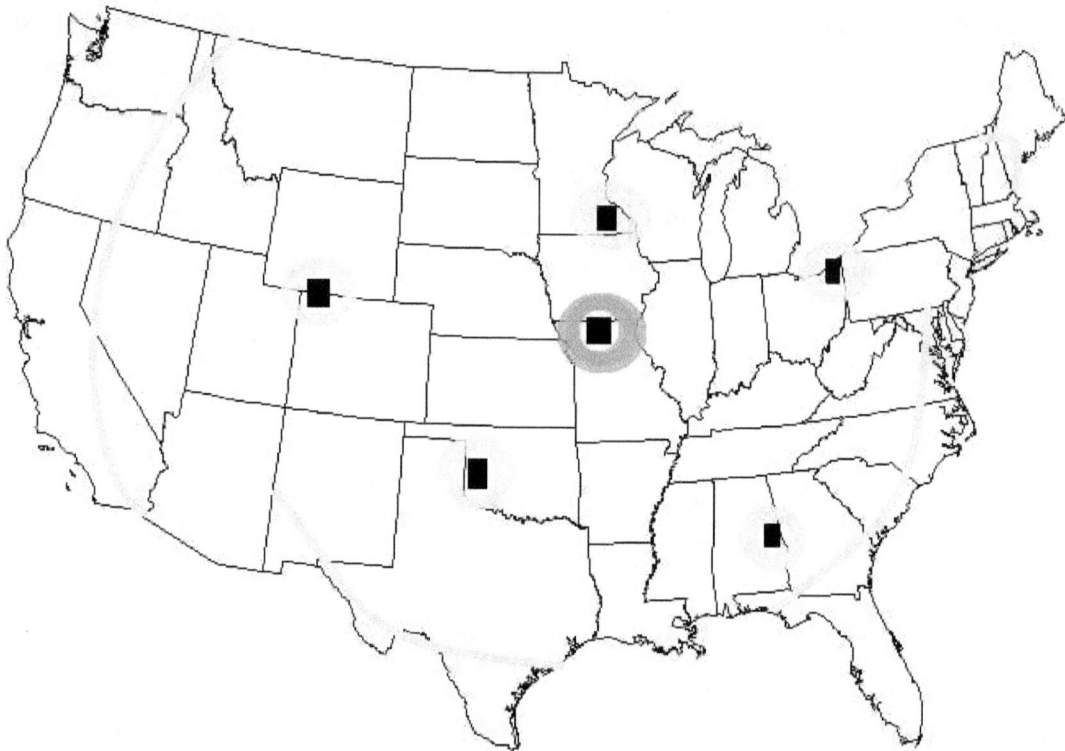

Using "Superstorm Sandy" as an example, C-130s stationed at Scott AFB would have about a four hour flight to the New York tri-state area. Therefore, the initial 75 C-130s would deliver their initial payloads in staggered time interval loads (45,000 lbs. per plane) and then depart to Wright – Patterson AFB (Ohio: closest permanent secondary re-supply center). In general terms, there would be two cargo trips in half the time and distance rather than using Scott AFB as secondary supply center. It should be noted that the C-130 can also land at most municipal airports in a given area. Bill reaffirmed his scenario by stating he had managers at Microsoft do a computer simulation of the storm relief process and found the system sound and worthy of installing.

Bill, upon rendering the above analysis, specifically addressed the President and General Skoler in terms of the total C-130s and the 75 proposed as needed for a domestic disaster. Bill was quick to state that assigning 92 C-130s to Operation LifeSaver would still maintain the necessary humanitarian efforts needed in the United States.

In addition, C-17 Globe Master IIIs could supplement C-130s. They may be limited in use because only 250 were manufactured since 1991 and runway requirements are twice that of the C-130s. Use of C-17 is particularly helpful in aiding the air lift of supplies because their payload is four times the amount of a C-130.

In addition to using C-130s in a disaster, reliance must be placed upon Boeing's 747-400F and 747-8F to deliver 295,800 lbs. of cargo per plane, per trip. <u>Deliverance</u> is imperative!! In addition, Bill stated that almost all of the 747s should come from commercial carriers (e.g., UPS) and have contingent emergency plans also in conjunction with the American Red Cross and the National Guards. Bill also advocated that the 747 carriers should donate their plane services with cargo from other sources, if possible. In turn, the carriers who volunteer their services would be given widespread television recognition of their efforts (indirect advertising) from charitable oriented TV networks. Unlike the C-130 runway requirements (3,586 ft.) the 747s require a minimum runway of greater than 11,000 ft. In addition, the 747s cannot air-drop supplies or manpower from the aircraft during flight.

Use of military C-5s and C-17s would also be instrumental as freight planes due to their cargo specifications.

General Skoler said he would need time to consider Bill's plan and confer with his air force advisories, the American Red Cross and National Guard, all of which would probably take the better part of two weeks in his estimate.

"Mr. President," Bill stated, "when the Musketeers were at Davis-Monthan Air Force Base counting B-52s, General Skoler said with your orders, 62 B-52s could be airworthy and delivered to Operation LifeSaver. At the moment, General Skoler said the non-current F and G series of B-52s could be converted to drop supplies with pin point accuracy."

President Obama said, "We will have to confront the Russians in relationship to the SMART disarmament treaty and Operation LifeSaver. For the best interests of all involved, the aircraft could be inspected by U.N. personnel periodically. Conversion costs, to drop supplies, for the total 62 aircraft would range about $15,287,000." Melinda, in all earnestness, said, "The B-52s would be converted from a military bomber to a peace provider."

President Obama said he will negotiate with the Russians with respect to the B-52s upon the onset of Operation Lifesaver.

Changing the subject, I indicated to the Summit members that once we have a firm handle on both the decommissioned and three commissioned carriers (presently being disarmed) and two amphibious assault ships, (also disarmed) we should allow 3-4 weeks for them to be primed and painted white with red crosses.

I also noted, in relationship to the ships used in Operation LifeSaver, that international law permits hospital ships to arm themselves with defensive weapons and deterrents. Such armament, in my opinion, is necessary due to the privateering of ships in recent years. The definition of defensive weapons should be set forth by the United Nations quickly, in order that completion and disembarkment dates are not delayed!!! All members of the Summit were in agreement with my suggestion.

President Obama stated with a reservation in his demeanor. He stated he has contacted select African county leaders and there was an apprehension to locate an air force base in their country. No country had a reservation with Operation LifeSaver medical carriers, airlifting helicopters, and medical C-130s, for aiding the treatment of the medically sick (including malnourishment). <u>These statements were reassurance of former phone calls made by the President on the onset of Operation LifeSaver.</u> President Obama said he and Mrs. Obama are going to make a personal visit to each country he recently contacted. The President noted to the members of the Summit, that using large military cargo planes may have the connotation that they may be used in a military assault. This misconception can hopefully be resolved by the United Nations.

The President repeated his former statement that the only way Operation LifeSaver will be viable is with the United Nations acceptance and participation in the plan. The <u>non-African</u> selected nations will be called upon by retired Admiral Mike Mullen, Melinda, Bill and I. Contacts will begin as early as next week to procure international participation by approval with country leaders and contributed pledges of support. President Obama said, after his first African phone contact, he stopped mentioning use of B-52s until the plan is fully accepted and operational with participating countries. The President's staff immediately contacted Davis-Monthan Air Force Base to stop the B-52s conversion to deliver supplies, for the time being.

Accordingly, The President will make a visit to each African country he chose, within a week, with hopes of establishing a centrally located air force base for all military <u>freight</u> planes. Further, there was no reluctance as to the 747s, if inspected by UN officials prior to take-off. The President also stated he selected countries along the Central and lower Western Atlantic coastal regions for his consideration. The following countries were his choice of nations:

- GHANA
- NIGERIA
- GABON

- TOGO
- CAMEROON

- BENN
- EQUALTORIAL GUINEA

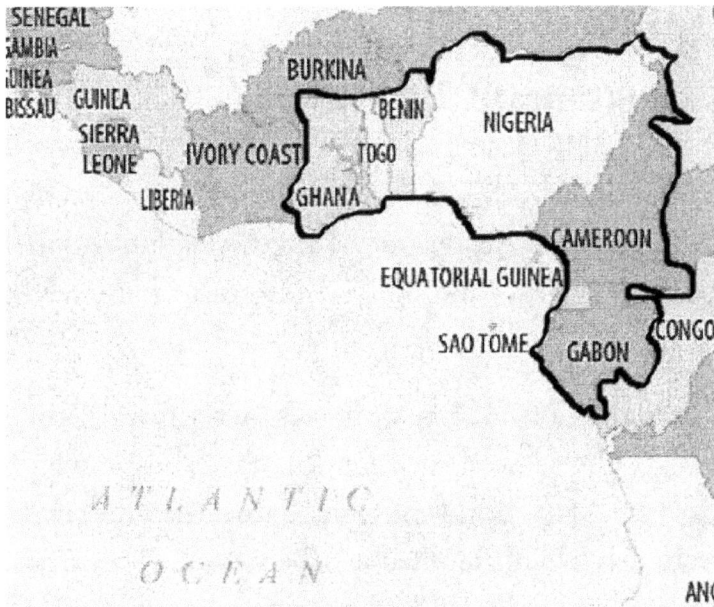

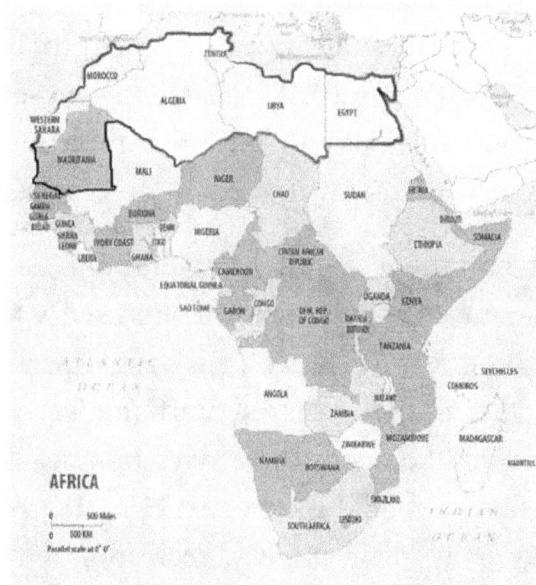

South of accented line is the Sub-Saharan desert.

President Obama concluded he was most interested in English speaking nations, particularly Nigeria with their massive population and acceptance of English as their official language. He also felt he had a very good rapport with President Goodluck Jonathan of Nigeria; President Paul Biya (Head of State) and Prime Minister Phile'mon Yang (Head of Government) of Cameroon; and President John Dramani Mahama of Ghana. President Obama was hopeful for the ones just noted, or any other nation he contacted. Summit Two concluded after nine hours of diligent work and a sense of purpose by each member.

The Paltz and Gates Foundation
Washington, D.C.

The Musketeers arrived at the Foundation at 7:00 a.m. with some aches and pains from sitting so long at the Summit yesterday. When getting out of the Gates limousine, both Bill and Melinda had to each grab one of my arms and pull me out on to the street. I was able to walk with a "clink" in my back.

My agenda for the day was clear – monitor naval ships' progress with four of my ship managers. Before our ship meeting, I reviewed dozens of faxes that were unanswered in the near past. Retired Captain Matt Bonds informed me that the two amphibious assault ships in our plan were having difficulties of their own. The USS Tarawa, presently located near Pearl Harbor, is being considered to become a museum. I immediately called our contact at the White House and explained the USS Tarawa's museum situation and the impact it is having in our restoration process. The USS Nassau, stationed at Beaumont, Texas, is also progressing behind schedule and needs a strict examination of their PERT charts to determine why there is a possible delay in their commission date. Within an hour of my contact with the White House, I received a fax to continue as necessary to meet our commission date.

During the week following Summit Two, the Musketeers and Mike Mullen worked on their contact and protocol to be used when addressing Presidents and Ministers of foreign countries. Mike, with his vast experience at international relations gained when Chairman of Joint Chiefs of Staff (under two administrations), was invaluable to the Musketeers. Mike spent three days briefing us on how to properly address a country's leader. Mike said a Musketeer will get a profile of past and present accomplishments, contributions to their country, recreation, enjoyment, family, etc. A government agency will supply this information. This background is necessary in selling Operation LifeSaver to a potential participant. Stay away from viewpoints that could have adverse effects (like Religion). Remember to be yourself and that you are acting solely as a humanitarian to procure life for millions of people who must be treated medically, nutritionally, economically, educationally, and socially. Africa, as addressed by the three Musketeers, is <u>not</u> a seemingly impossible task, even though complicated, and can be a challenge to millions of individuals who have the will and leadership to advocate human rights needed so desperately. Since many on the non-African countries were previously assigned, a new "shuffling of the cards" was necessary.

Chris	Russia, United Kingdom, Norway, Sweden, etc.
Bill	France, Switzerland, China, India, Cambodia, etc.
Melinda	Canada, Japan, Australia, Philippines, New Zealand, etc.
Mike	Germany, Turkey, Spain, Italy, and numerous smaller countries.

The White House
Washington, D.C.

The President called a brief meeting at the White House to report his and Mrs. Obama's trip to Africa last week. He stated they were able to gain the acceptance of two air force bases for transportation of supplies not only to their individual countries, but other countries participating in Operation LifeSaver. The news was well received with a round of applause and relief by all members present. Both Nigeria and Gabon consented to the building of an air base for approved military freight planes (carrying medical supplies, food, water, trucks, and construction equipment), etc. I stated that since our ships were for the most part at the painting stage, it is appropriate to start our negotiations to gain support for Operation LifeSaver. Bill added "his" aircraft were also in the painting stage, too.

The President said he was sure that the Musketeers and retired Admiral Mullen would gain support and he had full confidence in our abilities to accomplish our mission. Bill noted that Microsoft was underway in starting **Division Two** and was to be operating formally within the next two weeks!!! Everyone at the meeting was still amazed at Bill's ambition and use of Microsoft's resources to create a solution to Africa's starvation situation.

Melinda was next to speak and said she was working on the economy and the impure water situation on a constant basis and was eager to inform the committee of her findings to date. The President was anxious to hear Melinda's findings, but they would have to be put on hold for the time being. Melinda replied that she fully understood and had a mountain of work ahead that the Musketeers really had to address as a team, in any case.

International Negotiations
FRANCE
Bill Gates

Bill leased a jet, as charitable expense, to fly to Paris, France – his favorite wine country. Bill was formally greeted by President Francios Hollande and Prime Minister Jean-Marc Ayralt at the Paris airport. After a half an hour of greetings the brigade of limousines departed – Bill to the Hotel Meurice. After a two hour rest in his hotel room, Bill met with the United States Ambassador to France, Charles Rivkin, in the restaurant Le Meurice. Bill talked about Operation LifeSaver over a bottle of Chateau Rayas wine ($800 a bottle in American currency) during their dinner. Ambassador Rivkin was taken aback that the Musketeers have taken upon themselves to address the African situation at all. Bill stated it is the Musketeers destiny in life to have the satisfaction of saving millions of lives, challenging all challenges, with a sense of happiness and a good laugh or two along the way. The Musketeers have incorporated the use of converted aircraft carriers and amphibious assault ships into naval medical ships and recycled aircrafts, along with a system to disburse supplies even to the remotest parts of the countries presently being addressed. We know we can turn this horrible (holistic) situation around within our lifetime. The feat is _not_ impossible, as so many people think. The dinner ended with a parfait and a firm hand shake upon departure.

The very next day, Bill met with the President and Prime Minister of France to discuss only Operation LifeSaver. Bill discussed the plan in humanitarian aspects, with the need of transportation assets, manpower and monetary assistance. The appeal was earnest and well received by the two leaders. President Hollande stated they would have to inventory assets and get a government vote on monetary aid. President Hollande said France has a long history with numerous African countries, as noted by French as their official language, and are extremely interested in giving aid to as many African countries as possible. Both individuals said "off the record," they would give it their best efforts to gather significant funds for the plan now and in the years to come.

Bill departed with vast hopes of support from the French government.

Next, Bill was off to Switzerland by train – more exciting travel before he leaves for Cambodia!

International Negotiations
CANADA
Melinda Gates

Melinda's first stop for negotiations was Canada.

Melinda, by chance, was able to visit Ottawa, the capital of Canada, when both Queen Elizabeth II and Prime Minister Stephen Harper were available for a meeting concerning Operation LifeSaver.

Melinda, upon reaching Ottawa by bus, took a cab to the Holiday Inn nearest the Parliament complex. The next morning after breakfast in the lobby of the Holiday Inn, she grabbed a cab to Parliament for her audience with the leadership of Canada. Queen Elizabeth II (the Constitutional Monarch) and Prime Minister Harper personally greeted Melinda upon her arrival. After an hour of "shooting the breeze," namely about the Montreal Canadians hockey team and the past Olympic games, the threesome settled down to discuss Operation LifeSaver. Melinda described the commitment the United States has assembled for the African cause in terms of manpower, converted aircraft carriers, two hospital ships, aircraft, and six additional examples of humanitarian relief to the Sub-Sahara region of Africa. Melinda stated that Africa (truly an international venue to direct aid to these most deprived people) is plagued by disease, starvation, impure water and social injustice. Melinda further stated that she was a partner in the management of the plan along with her husband Bill, and the world famous Certified Public Accountant, Christopher Paltz; collectively known as the Musketeers.

Before Melinda departed she was pledged that Operation LifeSaver would be brought before Parliament and voted upon for extending manpower and all important monetary assistance. The meeting went extremely well and Melinda was on her way to Japan for her next Operation LifeSaver negotiation.

The White House
Washington, D.C.

President Obama asked Mike Mullen and I for a private meeting. Bill and Melinda were on their negotiation tours already. I picked up Mike at the train station in my 1963 Corvette Stingray. Mike was surprised that I maintain such a "sporty image" being 66. I "burnt rubber" leaving the train station to make sure that Mike was wide awake and ready for our meeting with the President. The President was glad to see us as we met in the Oval Office. President Obama was quick to ask Mike if he would officially return to active duty at his former rank as a four star Admiral. Mike replied he thought he would be asked to return with the development of Operation LifeSaver being executed in its initial stages, and that he regrets he has only two lives to give to his country. With a smile, the President shook Mike's hand and then gave him a new set of four star insignias.

Mike said, at this point, he was annoyed with the FBI insinuating he was doing something wrong when they removed his computers from his office and personal residence. The only explanation the FBI gave "is that it was very serious."

"Mr. President, what the heck going on here? I served a most honorable career and gave my job the very best I could in my service to our country. The Special Agents were, in all likelihood, misled by their superiors. I cannot permit this type of insinuation!!!"

The President said "I was notified of these actions by the Washington Post and immediately got to the bottom of these events."

"There was a severe error and confusion in the whole matter and you were erroneously mistaken for a possible breakdown in internal control that never existed. I will personally assume responsibility for your character and accusations against it, as well for the Musketeers."

"Thank you, Mr. President."

"Before I forget Mike, would you wear your dress white uniform when doing your negotiations?"

"Yes, Mr. President."

"Mike, before you return to Washington D.C., I think a visit to NATO headquarters would be appropriate to inform them of Operation LifeSaver and our approach to the African plan spearheaded by the Musketeers and accepted by the United

States in a monumental way. African nations, while not a member of NATO could be strategically influenced by NATO countries when naval and air forces are actively participating without United Nations, American, and Russian approval.

"Chris," the President said, "we have two administrative matters to consider before you depart on your negotiations. First, I want as many health carriers to depart at the same time, loaded with helicopters, partially disassembled (e.g., without corresponding rooters attached), maximum supplies and fully manned. Second, Chris, my staff contacted the American Medical Association and they granted the time working with African patients toward their internship or residency. In addition my staff contacted "Doctors Without Borders" and they are ecstatic that Operation LifeSaver would serve so many individuals in Africa and they are definitely interested in volunteering on board of our health carriers or assessment ground stations.

"Mr. President," I asked, "have we heard from the United Nations to get their acquiescence for defensive armament on our ships, while under restoration and before crossing the Atlantic?"

"No, Chris," answered the President, "I stated if ships are armed vessels, beyond defensive weapons, they can lose their status as a hospital ship under international law. If unarmed, we are subject to privateering and other potential harm. Also, waiting for the United Nations to respond will delay our entire schedule for completion and departure of our fleet. I will contact John Ashe (President of the United Nations General Assembly) for an immediate reply and resolution."

As a side note, I stated that painting ships white will be visible to spectators shortly. "We must co-ordinate the announcement of Operation LifeSaver with public awareness and interest." I also stated that I have given the orders to activate the USS Mercy hospital ship in San Diego and have the ship proceed to Norfolk Naval Base."

We see the light at the end of the railroad tunnel, rather than the darkness of a cave. Once our negotiations start to generate funds, even from deficit countries, they will all be contributing funds toward operating expenses and will also be able to embark on our humanitarian plan –

> Americans must always be willing to think, think and think until this horrible Holocaust is over!!!

> Americans must lay down weapons and fight, fight, fight until this horrible Holocaust is over!!!

Americans must give, give, give wholeheartedly, as in WWII, until this horrible Holocaust is over!!!

"Mr. President," I injected, "happy are the men and woman that have a spray gun or a paint brush in their hand – perhaps, they will never find a happier time in their lives, than now in using white paint, for such an important purpose, as Operation LifeSaver.

"Day-by-day," I continued, "we watch the clock tick down until the fleet of hospital ships are ready to embark. Helicopters will have their rotors removed, until the coast of Africa is in sight. The helicopters are presently being delivered by train to Norfolk Naval base. Bill and I are in constant contact with our ship and aircraft volunteer managers at the Foundation and Pentagon. The Musketeers are anxious: three months of work and preparation are in abeyance."

International Negotiations
GERMANY
Admiral Mullen

Admiral Mike Mullen chose Germany as his first nation to negotiate with.

Recently, the capital of Germany was moved from Bonn to Berlin. The choice of Bonn goes to post WWII when the Soviet Union occupied East Germany and East Berlin.

Admiral Mullen had many thoughts on his mind during his flight from Washington, D.C. to Berlin, Germany. First memories of visiting German extermination camps and how they paralleled the dead in Africa resurfaced. He could not accept the fact that these conditions existed today, and, although not the result of a particular country, are allowed to exist by the world-at-large. Mike could not keep out of his mind the need for Germany to give "pay-backs" (ask for, and may be given absolution) for their past country crimes against humanity when the Nazi party murdered millions of the beautiful Jewish congregation in Germany and occupied counties during WWII.

Germany must make penance for their previous mortal sins or be shunned by the religious community in America and the world. Lack of action by the Germans would also be considered another crime against humanity. Mike was increasingly upset, and rightfully so!!!

Mike, by chance, remembered when Chris mentioned something about how catching terrorists, criminals, family deserters, illegal aliens and serious motor vehicle violators failed because he required a bounty for each violation – I must ask him about this when I see him again.

Admiral Mullen was given all the formalities upon his arrival to Berlin and would meet with the President and Chancellor of Germany the next morning. After a few hours of rest Mike met with the American Ambassador to Germany, John Emerson at Berlin's USO. After two Cokes each, they ordered. Mike ordered a California cheeseburger and John a pasta dish. Mike asked John about Germany's aid to sub-Sahara countries. John answered that it is considered low. Germany and many European countries complain that the recipients of the aid rely on funds solely and stop working. Many others say that the natural resources are exported out of the continent – fish, oil, minerals – and potential products lie idle and not manufactured. As you know the roadways are practically non-existent and modern equipment is but a dream. Mike indicated the initial stages of Operation LifeSaver are well under way. Medical care is first and foremost which we have extensively addressed. Extensive use of helicopters will be underway when medical ships are strategically situated. Presently, we have commitments for ten formerly active military naval ships, and two United States Naval Hospital Ships. Work on the ships is presently on schedule and will be medically sea-worthy within a month.

"I wish you well in the morning, Admiral Mullen."

"Thanks, John."

"FIGHT" AT THE O.K. CORRAL:

When Admiral Mullen entered the meeting room there was a silence…

Both the President Joachim Gauck and Chancellor Angela Merkel rose from their seats and greeted Admiral Mullen with a hand shake. All three immediately seated themselves. Both leaders spoke fluent English. Chancellor Merkel spoke first. She stated she was briefed on Operation LifeSaver from France's President. Based upon Chancellor Markel's "briefing statement," Admiral Mullen, without hesitation, addressed her with the following questions and also gave the following counter- replies:

"Do you know who founded the Paltz and Gates Foundation?" "NO," she replied.

"Bill and Melinda Gates and the world famous Certified Public Accountant, Christopher Paltz did," stated Admiral Mullen.

"Do you know how many navy ships will be in the medical fleet?" "NO," she replied.

"Twelve," stated Admiral Mullen.

"Do you know if medical doctors can do their residency on a medical carrier?" "NO," she replied.

"Yes, with the acquiescence of the AMA and required course work," stated Admiral Mullen.

"Do you know what coastal regions of Africa are being treated first?" "NO," she replied.

"The lower and central coastal sections," stated Admiral Mullen.

"Do you know if North and South Korea will be asked to participate? "NO," she replied.

"Yes, but in different sections," stated Admiral Mullen.

"Do you know that there are detailed plans for transporting patients to medical carriers?" "NO," she replied.

"Yes, very much so," stated Admiral Mullen

"Do you know that the United States is donating ten of its aircraft carriers? "NO," she replied.

"Yes," stated Admiral Mullen.

"Do you know, as we speak, that the medical carriers are being painted white with red crosses?" "NO," she replied

"Yes, by volunteers under the supervision of naval personnel," stated Admiral Mullen.

"Do you know that it is the hopes of the plan that the USA and Russia will manage the African transition?" "NO," she replied.

"Yes, Operation LifeSaver is extremely hopeful that there will be a co-mingling of humanitarian understandings, even with different ideologies, toward a common goal of serving mankind," stated Admiral Mullen.

ADMIRAL MULLEN SAID TO HIMSELF:

FOLKS YOU HAVE JUST BEEN FRIED!!!

Mike further stated, "I am here as a representative of the United States and, specifically Operation LifeSaver. The founders, who are also quasi-Generals, were appointed by the President of the United States to command the conversion of Africa from a diseased state of being, to healthy countries asking for help when only absolutely necessary to maintain their social stability and medical soundness.

Transformation from a disease state to a responsible self-sustaining state is totally possible with sound management of manpower. Christopher Paltz will chair the financing of the project. As presently planned, each country of need will be assigned a finance committee of no less than ten renowned CPAs to address hands-on reform where necessary, and adherence to international funding regulations. Bill Gates will chair communications and direct veterans who have expertise in the communication and computer fields. Melinda will oversee Human Relations and directing of long term planning as though it were a short term project.

"Operation LifeSaver's appeal to the German people is to recognize the holocaustic conditions existing in Africa today and how it is reminiscent of WWII treatment of the Jewish population. Americans feel that the German population of today must make restitution of their forefather's execution of millions of Jewish individuals in the holocaust that was existent during WWII. It is not beyond our expectations that Germany will provide the most respective manpower and greatest financial aid than any other nation in the world!!!

"Now, before it is too late, you must consider redemption and act upon it.

America will be waiting your decision!!!"

Admiral Mullen rose and left without another word.

Speech
Admiral Mullen
NATO Headquarters
Brussels

The skies were blue with mild clouds blocking the sun on occasion. Admiral Mullen was like when General George Patton addressed the Third Army in England during WWII. He spoke distinctly into four microphones to an audience of 5,000 NATO workers in the parking lot of NATO Headquarters. The message, while lasting 42 minutes, was clear to every attendant, that the United States, through the Musketeers, was openly addressing the 21st century holocaust that exists in Africa. Admiral Mullen addressed the action already taken by the United States and current negotiations to raise funds and manpower to back up the plan.

American Normandy Military Cemetery
France
Admiral Mullen
Christopher Paltz

Before Admiral Mullen departed home to the United States and Christopher's negotiations with the Russians, both individuals met in the Memorial Chapel at Normandy, France. At this point in time, there was no time... only time to rest forever in the earth once walked upon by American soldiers who gave their life for freedom, liberty, the right to fall in love with their loved ones, and their beloved country called the United States of America. It was the Creator's wishes that over 9,400 American soldiers would sacrifice their lives in the humbling of his wishes. Admiral Mullen and Christopher prayed in the Chapel before embarking on the forever hollowed grounds where so many are buried. There is no way, in writing, that can relay our feelings and tears in our eyes as we walked up and down rows of Crosses and Star of Davids. At one point we placed each of our hands on a monument and knelt in prayer. I witnessed this site once and will return. I must also pray at the hollow grounds of Lorraine, Brittany and Epinal amongst others, in the immediate future.

We departed our separate ways after a hearty hand shake.

JAGUAR E-TYPE (XKE)

International Negotiations
Russia
Christopher Paltz

I rented a Jaguar E-Type (XKE) for my ride from Paris to Moscow. The XKE was a convertible and complimented my "sporty image" and taste in cars. I was in no hurry and needed time to think about my presentation to Vladimir Putin and Dmitry Medvedev on Tuesday. Upon arriving in Moscow I proceeded to the United States Embassy, where I would dine and spend the night. Ambassador Michael McFaul, upon hearing my XKE pull up, greeted me at the door. I immediately said I must use the Men's room, as so many travelers do.

After a two hour rest, my presence at diner was requested. The meal for the night was corned beef and cabbage – my favorite. After dinner Michael and two other embassy officials sat down with me to discuss Operation LifeSaver. After our informative discussions, the Ambassador and his staff were fully updated on the plan.

At 10:00 a.m., I met with President Vladimir Putin and Chairman of the Government Dmitri Medvedev. An interpreter reduced any possible misconceptions due to language differences. After formalities, lasting half an hour, we addressed Operation LifeSaver. My initial approach was to discuss the tragedies of WWII and the war with the Nazis. Then I came directly to the point of the Holocaust presently existing in Africa. My discussion also stated that the United States has converted ten ships into "Medical Carriers." For the next 45 minutes, I addressed the subject in greater depth and emotion.

President Putin excused himself and returned shortly with General Devmied of the Russian Air Force.

"Based upon your presentation of Operation LifeSaver, Christopher," stated President Putin, "Russia is in position to donate seed money (start-up funds), in the amount of one billion [U.S. dollars]. Now is no better time than ever to amalgamate relations between Russia and the United States."

I stated our two countries would work together to monitor the operating aspects of Operation LifeSaver until a country's self-sufficiency is attained. The Musketeers, once the alliance materializes, would also address the non-operating aspects of Operation LifeSaver – other lifesaving situations facing the continent.

President Putin addressed his quasi-military plan, which took half an hour to explain. I immediately said to President Putin, that, as a representative of the United States, inclusion of a B-2 Stealth Bomber would not be feasible. I did say, however, I would relay a <u>revised plan</u> (w/o the B-2) to President Obama, Bill and Melinda Gates, Admiral Mullen and the Joint Chiefs of Staff.

My "gut feeling" was to not discuss any aspect of using B-52s in our initial talks with the Russians. Yes! At another point in time!

I was ready to leave when President Putin said "where are you going? Let me show you the Kremlin and some other sites." I was surprised, but eager to accept his invitation. After touring the Kremlin and two museums, President Putin stated his staff noticed I was driving an Jaguar XKE – "I like your 'sporty image,' Christopher." How about taking me up with a sport?"

"How about darts?"
He replied. "NO, NO."
"Do you have bowling in Russia?"
"YES, YES. Let's GO, GO…"

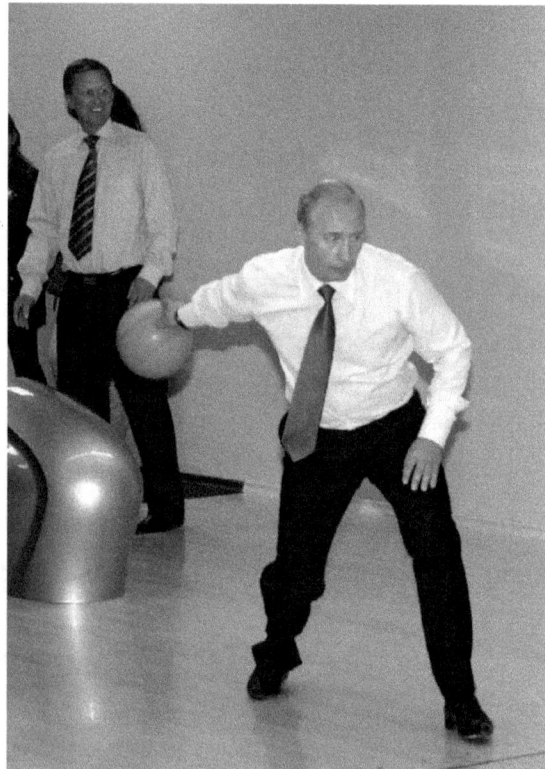

Photo Source: http://widelec.org/p/3852/super-putin/3/

PRESIDENT PUTIN BOWLS WITH CHRISTOPHER AFTER OPERATION LIFESAVER NEGOTIATIONS

Once we reached the bowling alley, I was going to tell President Putin that I had a scholarship for bowling in college – but I didn't. We each won two games and were about to face the tie breaker. After picking up my ball and was ready to make my approach, I turned and set my ball down. "Let's call it quits while even and say we're friends!!!" At that point, we departed with a hardy hand shake. President Putin said he hopes to hear from the United States soon.

The White House
Washington D.C.

Summit Three

The President, Musketeers, Admiral Mullen and the Joint Chiefs of Staff met in our usual conference room in the White House. President Obama said he heard from the Germans and they would top any monetary assistance pledged, and they raised over 5,237 volunteers to date. Admiral Mullen said he was very <u>firm and sincere</u> with the leadership of Germany (I remember Mike's interview with "Harvard Business Review," where he was quoted that you must "be very sincere" in your career…) Admiral Mullen was true to his word, as with the Germans. The President was particularly pleased with the German pledge.

The Gates also found major pledges in their negotiations, too.

Next was my turn. I reported my successes in Europe…

THEN, I MADE MY PRESENTATION ABOUT MY MEETING WITH THE RUSSIANS.

I said the Russians pledged $1,000,000,000 (U.S. Dollars) if there was a show of faith between our countries. "President Putin stated we must engage in a peaceful qusi-military maneuver over the Mediterranean Sea. His plan is to have a supersonic bomber from Russia and United States meet over the Mediterranean Sea flying at only 500 mph in a figure eight. Once flying three figure eights the bombers would invert their position and follow the other aircraft for another three additional figure eights. The specific aircraft would be the Russian supersonic bomber Tupolev Tu-160 and the American supersonic bomber Rockwell B-1B lancer. Upon completion of the two sets of three figure eights both aircraft would fly to Geneva, Switzerland to celebrate and show the world that the two greatest world powers would actively participate in Operation LifeSaver."

All members present at Summit Two were extremely surprised and taken aback.

President Obama, after clearing his throat, said this is unheard of, but would show that both our intentions are of the highest and noblest in the world.

"However, there is a 'catch' to this whole proposal," I said. "President Putin wants me as a non-operating co-pilot in a Russian Tu-160 bomber and Bill as a non-operating co-pilot in an American B-1B bomber. Bill, while almost falling out of his chair, ran to the men's room and slammed the door!!!

President Obama said it was time to formally address American citizens and the world about Operation LifeSaver. At 9:00 p.m., the President revealed the plan in specific terms on national TV from the White House. He concluded that Christopher Paltz and Bill Gates consented to the Russian aircraft proposal, only after the one billion dollar Russian pledge was deposited in the World Bank for Operation LifeSaver. Finally the President noted we cannot live in prosperity while a holocaust continues to exist. It was the allied troops who liberated the beautiful Jewish people that were left in Germany's reign in WWII. Now it is time for the world to liberate the beautiful citizens of Africa.

The White House
Washington, D.C.
Recognition – Diplomacy

Once again, President Obama invited the Musketeers and Admiral Mullen to the White House for a meeting. We met in the Oval office. "Bill and Chris," said President Obama, "you are about to embark on a very dangerous mission for the world. Finally, the United States Senate and House have agreed on something!!! Congress voted Bill, Melinda and me to the position of Five Star General – usually awarded only in times of war." The President opened a case and pinned the five star insignia on each of our collars. I asked the President who has the greater authority amongst us? We all had a laugh.

President Obama quickly changed the subject. He said he contacted President Putin and we agreed that it would be in the best interest of our countries to have both Presidents present when the supersonic bombers arrive in Geneva. Both Presidents, representing vast populations, would project a possible alliance that existed during WWII.

"Even though the United States and the Soviet Union were at odds during the Cold War, the prospects of leadership and alliance between our countries will never, in my opinion, be greater than now," stated President Obama.

Melinda added, "it is really time we freed our countries of the political Holocaust that exists even until today, too. I remember studying when Clara Barton [the first President of the American National Red Cross] was awarded the Silver Cross of Imperial Russia for supplies extended during the famine of 1892. Certainly, if the American Red Cross was willing to extend humanitarian help to Russia in 1892, we are in the position to unify our efforts, with Russia, in resolving the African holocaust and commence a lasting, civilized, sincere, and friendly relationship between our two countries."

The topic changed again when I said I had an idea that we give out a hand held (15") stick pole with both the American and Russian flags attached to the same pole. Melinda also added that the numbers of spectators are multiplying five-fold each day to see where the B-1B bomber will take off. There was enough time to fly "UPS" flags to Switzerland and Russia in order to have them available a day before take-off. The flags were ready on Wednesday before the flight and given out to all spectators who assembled at Dyess AFB – several hundred people were allowed closer to the field due to the notoriety at hand. Flags waved earnestly with cheers as personnel passed by the viewing area. The feeling of excitement was growing in the spectators' minds.

The next morning, Bill and Melinda boarded their jet and flew directly from Washington D.C to Dyess Air Force Base, Texas.

Christopher boarded a non-stop flight on an charter plane to Rome, Italy. Upon arrival to Rome, a Russian military aircraft flew Chris to Engels Air Force Base, in Russia.

Dyess	Engels
Air Force Base	Air Force Base
Texas	Russia
Bill Gates	Christopher Paltz

Before Bill set foot in a B-1B Lancer bomber he was given three thorough medical exams. Three doctors examined him and found him in excellent health. Melinda said to the doctors, "ever since Chris engaged my husband in Operation LifeSaver he has been irregular in his bowel movements." This condition is fairly frequent and is commonly called "loose intestinal movements." Melinda, with joy in her face... said, "That means my husband will not fly in the B-1B Lancer this week."

"No, Mrs. Gates, it means he will have to take an oral intestinal medication to clear his bowels or a rectal enema. Either way, the President has ordered him to fly on Saturday, when there will be excellent TV coverage and where international contribution donors are available."

Meanwhile, Bill was fitted for his flight suit with his name monogrammed on it. In addition, the flight suit had five stars embroidered on top of each shoulder, similar to Christopher's. After two test flights in the non-operational co-pilot's seat, Bill was anxious to go!!! The pilot (Ken Wegner) had a "Nose Art" picture of Melinda, with her name, painted on both sides of the nose of the plane. The painted woman (Melinda) was in remembrance of when our WWII airmen painted woman and other symbols on their bombers.

Bill, before his Mediterranean flight, was asked to remain on the Dyess Air Force Base, and happily so. He met so many military personnel that he would never have met before and appreciated their efforts to protect our country. Entirely pleased with the experience thus far, including the test flight on the B-1B Lancer supersonic bomber, Bill was completely over his initial physical response. President Putin's idea of augmenting goodwill between the United States and Russia by use of the B-1B Lancer and Tu-160 aircrafts, was well received by all.

The United States Air Force command also announced that a B-1B Supersonic bomber with Bill Gates aboard would depart from Dyess Air Force base on Saturday. Its mission is to peacefully engage with a Russian supersonic bomber (Tu-160) over the Mediterranean with Christopher Paltz aboard to land in Geneva, Switzerland, the mission was now officially announced. While the number of days counted down before takeoff decreased, there was a larger and larger amount of spectators appearing each day (countercyclical effect). The same was true at the Russian and Swiss airports. Actually, the expected amount of spectators was growing so large that "Port–A-Johns" were brought in with expectation of Saturday's attendance.

Bill, while at Dyess AFB, was interviewed by four major TV stations – of course he continued to emphasize that the historic flight was for Operation LifeSaver and Russia's pledge to aid Africa and promote international goodwill, too. Bill also stated that the United States spent billions of dollars in converting ten Navy ships into "hospital carriers" for the desperate need of medical care in select Sub-Saharan countries in Africa.

Meanwhile, on the Eastern front, Chris was given two preparation flights on a Russian Tu-160 supersonic bomber (as a non-operating co-pilot) in preparation for Saturday's flight. Chris was constantly being interviewed by the Russian press. Chris' actions in the Russian Air Base were also televised on national news throughout the United States along with Bill's news commentaries and interviews – there has not been as much international excitement since the moon landing in 1969.

Saturday finally arrived!!! The spectators numbered in the range of over 7,000 at Dyess AFB, Texas. Flags were waving everywhere. As the B-1B Lancer bomber was pulled out of its hanger, Bill Gates and crew of three were greeted by volumous cheers…….. Then the gathered spectators sang the "Star Spangled Banner" and the

"Anthem of Russia" as they waved to the crew. As the crew of four boarded the aircraft, the spectators chanted Go, Go, Go, Go……. After 15 minutes the crew's oxygen masks and head gear were in place, the 4 x "General Electric F101-GE-102 turbofan" engines were ready, and flight controls were checked twice; the aircraft was ready for takeoff. Bill and Ken Wegner (pilot) gave the spectators the thumbs up as the "B-1B Melinda" commenced its take-off. Spectators cheered as the flags waved and smiles abounded!!! TV cameras televised the B-1B take off until the aircraft was out of sight. Spectators were still waving their flags, patting each other on their backs as smiles were everywhere. Each person saw the historic lifetime event takeoff, with great patriotism and hope for the future prospects of ending the African holocaust and starting friendly relations with Russia. Many persons assembled were holding a cross or Star of David in prayer.

THE U.S. NATIONAL ANTHEM

"THE STAR SPANGLED BANNER"

(Written in 1814 by Francis Scott Key)

Oh, say can you see by the dawn's early light
What so proudly we hailed at the twilight's last gleaming?

Whose broad stripes and bright stars thru the perilous fight,
O'er the ramparts we watched were so gallantly streaming?

And the rockets' red glare, the bombs bursting in air,
Gave proof through the night that our flag was still there.

Oh, say does that Star - Spangled Banner yet wave
O'er the land of the free and the home of the brave?

ANTHEM OF RUSSIA

(Translation by Anastasia, 2004)

Russia ------- our sacred state,
Russia ------- our beloved country.
Might will-power, great glory
Shall remain your honors for all time

Praise our free Fatherland,
Long-lasting union of brotherly peoples,
Ancestor – given wisdom of the people!
Long live, Country! We are proud of you!

From the southern seas to the polar realm
Our forests and fields stretch.
You are one in the world! You are alone like that,
God-guarded native land!

Plenty of room for dreams and for life
The coming years are promising us.
Allegiance to our Motherland gives us strength.
So it had been, so it is, and so it always will be!

BILL GATES

ABOARD

"B-1B MELINDA"

UNITED STATES SUPERSONIC BOMBER

(as a non-operating co-pilot)

CHRISTOPHER PALTZ

ABOARD

Tu-160

RUSSIAN SUPERSONIC BOMBER

(as a non-operating co-pilot)

Chris was given a very similar take-off response from the Russian spectators, as the "B-1B Melinda" did in Texas. Viewers ranged around 6,700 and were very excited and vocal!! Immediately, before Chris and the other flight members boarded the Tu-160 aircraft both the Russian and American national anthems were sang. Spectators waved their "Russian /American" flags on the same stick and were ecstatic in respects to the upcoming flight and mission to help in the African Holocaust. Under the realm of the Soviet Union government, the coalition and international co-operation would not have been permitted or conceivable. However, people's thinking and attitudes can, and do, change in time, as evidenced by the show of good faith by both the Americans and Russians over a common cause.

The Russian Tu-160 took off without a hitch with Christopher Paltz on board (as a non-operating co-pilot). Time of takeoff and speed of the Tu-160 were predetermined to meet the "B-1B Melinda" at a specified coordinate over the Mediterranean Sea. Once in contact, both aircrafts did, as planned, three figure eights at 500 mph and then inverted their pattern to follow the other aircraft for an additional three figure eights and then fly, in formation, to Geneva. Each plane's crew was excited that everything went smoothly!!!

Now the real fun would begin at Geneva Airport when greeted by Presidents Obama and Putin and scores of diplomats from around the world. Two hours after the arrival of the bombers, there is a scheduled reception and most enthusiastic program at the "Grand Theatre of Geneva." The agenda at the "Grand Theatre" was to have both President Obama and President Putin give addresses on Operation LifeSaver and the progress by the United States and proposed use of the Russian aid. Extremely large screens were mounted so the audience could witness the descriptive aspects of Operation LifeSaver.

It was planned once the Presidents spoke; the Musketeers were also scheduled to make a presentation. Each Musketeer is to talk on how the plan was developed and their contributions to date. A Musketeer was scheduled for a fifteen minute address to the international congregation assembled at the "Grand Theatre." All plans were set, presentations prepared and attendants for the theatre were arriving early. Everything was running according to schedule, as excitement continued to grow throughout the Geneva Airport, the televised world, and the "Grand Theatre" – this was a true celebration in the making!!!

The first aircraft in sight was the white Russian Tupolev Tu-160 with Christopher aboard. Linda (Chris' "old" girlfriend) was present and so excited she literally jumped up-and-down with her hands covering her mouth in joy. The "White Swan," as Russians refer to the bomber on occasion, landed, taxied down the runway, and turned on to an auxiliary runway toward the airport terminal where she came to a stop from their part in the joint venture.

Melinda, while waiting for her husband to arrive on the "B-1B Melinda" bomber, was giving thought to issues that would be presented by the Musketeers at the "Grand Theatre" that very night:

- The "level-of-care" administered to a patient from beginning to end of treatment by Operation Lifesaver "system."
- Utilization of medical personnel as pertaining to "medical carriers," aircraft and land assessment stations.
- Building of rural "air-strips" for medical transportation.
- Many solutions to purifying water to drink, bath and medical purposes.
- Progression of Microsoft's multi-year food preservation program.
- Direct solutions to the construction of highways – intra/ international countries below the Sahara Desert.
- Earnest work for untold African citizens.
- A solution to housing and practical financing.
- American economic stimulus and excess employment.
- Balanced perspectives and monitoring by the United States and Russia until an African country is healthy and self-sufficient.
- Checks and balances between the United States and Russia monitoring, would be enhanced by United Nation contributions, too.

After a fifteen minute wait the "B-1B Melinda" was in sight and making her approach to the runway. As the tires touched down on the runway, <u>a large amount of black smoke emerged from the third turbofan engine!!!</u> Ken, the pilot, made a split second decision to land the aircraft, hoping the B-1B built in fire extinguishers would put out the engine's fire!!!

Smoke kept originating from the turbofan engine number three!!!

Panic broke out everywhere!!

President Obama and President Putin were "whisked" away in their respective limousine procession!!!

SMOKE CONTINUED FROM THE ENGINE NUMBER THREE!!!

WILL THE AMERICAN "B-1B MELINDA" BOMBER EXPLODE???

SMOKE CONTINUED FROM THE ENGINE NUMBER THREE!!!

FIRE CREWS PROCEEDED DIRECTLY TO THE BOMBER!!!

SMOKE CONTINUED FROM THE ENGINE NUMBER THREE!!!

While Bill's life and the crews are in danger,

Will they survive???

SMOKE CONTINUED FROM THE ENGINE NUMBER THREE!!!

Both bombers, according to the flight agreement, were to be empty of weapons. <u>Was the "B-1B Melinda" accidentally carrying explosives unaware to the crew???</u>

SMOKE CONTINUED FROM THE ENGINE NUMBER THREE!!!

SMOKE CONTINUED FROM THE ENGINE NUMBER THREE!!!

SMOKE CONTINUED FROM THE ENGINE NUMBER THREE!!!

SMOKE CONTINUED FROM THE ENGINE NUMBER THREE!!!

SMOKE CONTINUED FROM THE ENGINE NUMBER THREE!!!

SMOKE CONTINUED FROM THE ENGINE NUMBER THREE!!!

SMOKE CONTINUED FROM THE ENGINE NUMBER THREE!!!

SMOKE STARTED FROM THE ENGINE NUMBER FOUR!!!

!!! BAM !!!

!!! BAM !!!

POEM

OF THE

SOUL

My Vision...

My vision of the World extending itself to cure Africa, is priceless.

My vision of actually transforming the victims of needless horror to a bountiful life, is priceless.

My vision of worldly leadership extending their GOD given talent to a cause greater than themselves, is priceless.

My vision is to immediately transform the best aspects of our minds to new world leaders who will actually extend their hands beneath the soil of illness to the surface of new life granted by light and derived nourishment.

My vision is to immediately use the productive aspects of our mind to aid in propagating ideas and HOPE to millions of needy minds and bodies lost to neglect of the bountiful useless minds of affluence.

My vision is to beat the drum of silence so hard as to rip the canvas to shreds, as the blood of children, women and men are drained from the bottom of the drum onto the soil of famished crops.

My vision is to take a knife in hand and sever the vines choking the trees as it surrounds the base up onto limbs of so many... so many minds who are killed by vines.

My vision is to take clay and squeeze it in the palm of my hand until it secretes through my fingers to rest under my nails… only then will I know how to get my hands dirty as the clay hardens to rock.

My vision is to embrace those who minds will not astray by the wampum of yesterday.

My vision is to build a home that you can call your home, and not find it must fall behind in an unjust matter of time that will no longer be your own to look upon as home.

My vision is to take the needy and fill them with joy, as only a bright smile can. My bright smile of joy will find the needy frowning with the pain that joy cannot bring to their minds. Smiles are the result of an affluence of a kind, a kind not to kind to them, as they look upon a baby with a look of kindness from GOD, not to be confused with the smile of mankind.

My vision is to look at a zebra with stripes of a kind, to one day find, that I can ride that kind alongside of a palomino in stride, as graceful pastures remind me not to climb to far in time, only to find that I am writing a chime…

Christopher Paltz

Songs of the Soul

"PUT A LITTLE LOVE IN YOUR HEART"

Lyrics by Jackie Deshannon, 1968

Think of your fellow man
lend him a helping hand
put a little love in your heart.
You see it's getting late
oh please don't hesitate
put a little love in your heart.
And the world will be a better place
and the world will be a better place
for you and me
you just wait and see.

    Another day goes by
    and still the children cry
    put a little love in your heart.
    If you want the world to know
    we won't let hatred grow
    put a little love in your heart.
    And the world will be a better place
    and the world will be a better place
    for you and me
    you just wait and see.

        Take a good look around and
        if you're lookin down
        put a little love in your heart.
        I hope when you decide
        kindness will be your guide
        put a little love in your heart.
        And the world will be a better place
        and the world will be a better place
        for you and me
        you just wait and see
        put a little love in your heart...

THE END

of

I HAD A DREAM, TOO!!!

Chapter

CHAPTER VIII

<u>DISCLOSURE</u>

Since Bonnie, my wife and I led very private lives,
no one ever had a general idea of what our life
together was about. This was not intentional, just
the way it worked out. Even the closest to us knew
but a piece or two of the jigsaw puzzle. This text
is like a "private" corporation going "public" in a small
sense. I have provided a very short profile of Bonnie
and I before the text begins.

BONNIE DALE PALTZ

May 2, 1949

To

August 17, 2008

BONNIE

Raised in Meyersville, New Jersey, graduated Middlesex Hospital (NJ) School of Radiology as a "RT," she was on Social Security disability for decades. Bonnie was mobile and active, but had to be very careful not to put her back at risk (e.g., lifting heavy objects).

She had two Saint Bernards: Jager and Snoopes, at different times. The Saints lived with her parents in Meyersville and South Carolina. Bonnie needed extra cash just to get by these years of disability. She drove my mother, for one, to the store, bank, airport, Mom affectionately knew her as the "driver."

After a year of driving, we met and were brought together by our mutual love of Saint Bernards, -- attended our first dog show of Saints on our first date.

We were married after dating several years on October 22, 1995 at Schrewsburry Inn in NJ (A small but joyous affair). We lived in Cranford, NJ, for several years and then moved to Williams Township (Easton), PA, where we lived until Bonnie's death (8/17/08) and where I still live.

CHRISTOPHER

Born in Fanwood, NJ, graduated Pace University, School of Business, with a BBA and MBA, I am also a Certified Public Accountant (CPA). I worked for the firm of Alexander Grant, CPA's; Zimmermin Landscaping; Tri-Chem, Inc. (Hobby Craft Company), as a financial analyst; and the State of New Jersey (Department of Human Services) – Office of Auditing, as a financial auditor and administrator. Being an auditor, I also worked with the U.S. Attorney General (FBI), and the State of New Jersey Attorney General (Criminal Justice), on and off for many years. I audited nursing homes, hospitals, women's shelters, county seats, daycare centers, etc. – essentially wherever Federal and State money went to providing health care. My work as a health care auditor lasted over 20 years and I retired in 2004.

Memories of Bonnie and our lives together are like a bank vault. Imagine opening a bank safe and looking in and seeing thousands of boxes (all numbered and accessed only by key). Each box contains a memory--some good, some bad, some indifferent. Let us focus on six boxes that relate to Bonnie and I, randomly picked, to give you an idea why she was an excellent wife and "support team."

BOX 1022

This box is a large one filled with much happiness. Since Bonnie and I couldn't have natural children in our marriage due to medical reasons: one reason being it could have paralyzed Bonnie with her back disorder, we sought a surrogate.

Therefore, we traveled to Princeton, NJ and toured a St. Bernard kennel. We soon found out that we forgot just how big these "boys" were (200 lbs. plus) and how beautiful they looked. We saw a litter of puppies. One puppy came over to Bonnie. Bonnie picked him up and cradled him in her arms like a human baby. This was love at first sight (he looked like a stuffed dog does--so cute). Bonnie named him McKinley, McKinley Paltz. We purchased our baby, our happiness, our love until death did us part.

McKinley loved to eat, sleep, play, show affection, protect when necessary and have his tummy rubbed. Our baby grew, grew and grew until he reached adulthood. Let me tell you, he was no exception in his size and weighed in at 230 pounds of love.

I'll never forget one time, as an adult dog, McKinley was sitting in front of Bonnie (seated) with his right paw on her hand. Then McKinley turned his head toward me. I smiled and nodded my head up and down. McKinley turned his head to Bonnie and gave her the biggest kiss I've ever seen with his tongue. His tongue started under her chin, over her chin, lips, nose, brow and forehead. She wiped her brow and put her arms around his neck and "wrestled" all 230 lbs. of him to the carpet. At this time she immediately rubbed his tummy, and boy did he love that! So did she!

McKinley fit right in our home with a major medical disorder. He had epilepsy. At age two, he had his first seizure (he fell to the floor and his four legs moved as though he was running and he foamed at the mouth).

The seizures went on for about six months until I noticed that they occurred with major changes in atmospheric conditions. I went to the Internet (Allentown weather web site) and started plotting, on graph paper, five variables (indexes) in weather changes simultaneously. Basically, when the variables all "crisscrossed" each other, McKinley would seizure within an hour or two.

Predicting the seizure was only half the battle, treating them was the other half, I taped the windows air-tight in our computer room at home. When the crisscrossing occurred I would bring McKinley into the computer room, shut the door (with a draft stopper at the inside bottom of the door), and turn on two dehumidifiers. I would then plot on graph-paper every two hours the five variable movements until they all intersected again. At this point it was safe for us to turn off the computer and dehumidifiers and leave the room: seizure-free.

At the age 3+, McKinley had an unpredictable "grand" seizure in his bedroom on the second floor of our home. We summoned our vet and they came immediately. McKinley was in a coma and just breathing. It was too dangerous for us to carry him in our arms, plus his weight made carrying him impractical. Bonnie dialed 911 and summoned the Williams Township ambulance. The ambulance arrived and used their stretcher with McKinley strapped on, to bring him down the staircase and out to the vet's van. He was taken to the vets. Bonnie and I followed.

At the vets, McKinley was pronounced brain-dead. I rubbed his tummy and held his head at the same time. There was no movement. Bonnie stroked his coat and kissed him on the forehead for the very last time. We left the vets and our "baby" was soon put to sleep.

McKinley was cremated.

I buried his box of ashes in the garden (his yard) and had a small service for him. Bonnie, me, my children Rob, Suzanne Paltz and two neighbors (Brian and Maria) attended the service. Bonnie read the following passage from the bible:

"To everything there is a season, and a time to every purpose under the heaven:

A time to be born, and a time to die; A time to plant, and a time to pluck up that which is planted;

A time to kill, and a time to heal; A time to break down, and a time to build up;

A time to weep, and a time to laugh; A time to mourn, and a time to dance.

A time to cast away stones, and a time to gather stones together;

A time to embrace, and a time to refrain from embracing;

A time to get, and a time to lose; A time to keep, and a time to cast away;

A time to rend, and a time to sew; A time to keep silent, and a time to speak,

A time to love and a time to hate; A time of war, and a time of peace."

Ecclesiastes 3

Amen to a being, born in this world as a Saint; dying as innocent as when born; and fulfilling our need for a child in our marriage.

It's time now to slide Box 1022 back into the vault's memory spot where it belongs, turn the key, and move on.

BOX 1077

This box is a small one, but exemplary of my "sidekick."

This memory all started when I thought I would do artwork (I still do). The media was unique -- just go out on the interstate and you will find the highway littered with tire shreds of all different sizes and shapes.

Be that as it may, Bonnie and I headed out on Sunday mornings to collect various sizes and shapes of shredded tires on Route 78 in PA. Bonnie drove. I would get out of the car and pick up what I thought were unique pieces of tire and Bonnie would remain behind the wheel. While I was busy, trucks and cars were traveling at 80-90 mph only 20 feet away. The danger added a different dimension to the artwork: excitement!

The last time Bonnie and I went out, a state trooper pulled up behind us, with his flashing lights on, and he got out of his car. Our car's trunk was open with pieces of tire in it. The trooper looked around and said, "What's going on here?" I explained. He said "I am going to give you a ticket." "For what? We are not littering!" I said. "Try an unsafe move." He answered. I replied, "Giving my wife a ticket and points would be unjust because I directed her to drive. You can't give me a ticket because I'm not the driver."

Meanwhile, Bonnie got out of the car by passenger door and added, "I have been trying to get him to paint by numbers, but he says he has done that his whole career as a CPA." The trooper replied, "There is a dumpster at the Clinton Road Works with just shredded tires in it - go there and climb in all you want." We thanked him for his advice and he let us go.

When we got back into the car I commented to Bonnie, "I haven't jumped into a dumpster since I worked with the Attorney General." I think this tire hunt has gone far enough, let's go home, I have enough to work with."

Back goes Box 1077 with a twist of the key and we move on.

BOX 8741

This box holds but a drop of the memories I have about my brother Jonathan.

The phone rang at Bonnie's and my apartment in Cranford, NJ, one night many years ago. It was Jonathan. He said he went to the doctor and the doctor thought Jonathan had cancer of the lungs and liver and had only a short time to live. Bonnie and I immediately packed our bags, flew to Tampa, rented a car and drove to Plant City, where Jonathan lived. When we reached Plant City, Jonathan was already hospitalized in a very nice community-based hospital (a half mile from his home).

When Bonnie and I entered Jonathan's hospital room (at 7:00 p.m.), we found him lying in bed with the lights out, unshaven and a strong odor existed. Bonnie summoned the charge nurse to the room and demanded he be immediately bathed, shaved and given clean sheets.

At this time we queried the charge nurse about Jonathan's medical status. He was to be transferred to a "clinic" in Tampa for the destitute tomorrow. I replied that he was not to be moved until I spoke to the administrator in the morning. At 9:05 a.m. the next morning, we met with the administrator in her office. She told us he had to be moved to a Tampa "clinic" because he had no medical insurance. I replied "this is a community-based hospital and he has to be kept as a 'med-surge' patient — insurance or not -- it's in your charter." She replied, however, "our charter does not require the hospital to keep him as a long-term care unit patient," (nursing home type care).

The next day they operated on Jonathan's left lung and found it "black" from a lifetime of smoking. Blood tests also revealed a diseased liver. Jonathan was not long for this world.

Concurrently, Bonnie and I toured the geriatric ward in the hospital and found it excellent and about 75% occupied.

Then we proceeded to the comptroller's office and received a copy of their certified financial statements and the hospital's charter. The hospital was financially sound. The charter stated it had the option to accept geriatric patients or not.

The same day Bonnie and I toured a clinic in downtown Tampa. The clinic reeked of urine, stool and vomit. Most patients were on cots screaming (lack of medication), with puddles of urine beneath them and had unchanged diapers. We actually had to walk in puddles of urine to get to the admissions person. Being a field auditor for New Jersey nursing homes (ten years), I had never seen anything this bad in my career.

As Bonnie and I were exiting the clinic, Bonnie yelled, "Stop this! I can't take it." She then vomited her lunch on the sidewalk en route to Jonathan's car. Bonnie was pale and crying. "Is this what is going to happen to Jonathan?" I replied, "I don't know, I just don't know."

The next day we walked into Jonathan's room in the hospital and there was a woman present. We stared at one another and I said "Darlene?" She said, "Chris?" Yes. Yes. It was my cousin. I introduced her to Bonnie (it had been many years since I had last seen her). Darlene loved Jonathan very much. After Darlene was informed as to Jonathan's future, she said she would finance Jonathan's final days in a private nursing facility where Jonathan was going to spend his final days - Darlene was truly an Angel, Heaven sent.

Jonathan had <u>many</u> visitors before his passing; Walley, his brother; Dave, Darlene's brother; Carl, a friend from high school and roommate when Jonathan lived in New York City; etc., etc., (he had many friends in life).

Just two final notes… Jonathan died penniless… He was let go from his steady employment just before being vested into the pension plan, (he was a marketing manager). Jonathan was forced, as so many Americans are, to find any suitable kind of work at his age - he parked cars, painted, directed construction traffic, etc. to provide essential food and shelter.

Amazingly enough, he kept his personality right up to his final breath.

Back goes <u>Box 8741</u> with a twist of the key and we move on.

BOX 2227

This box has memories of Bonnie as a "Look-out."

The regional auditing office I worked out of was located in Greenbrook, NJ (in a noted state hospital for the mentally-challenged). The parking lot stretched from the administrative offices to a wooded area. One of our secretaries and another female social worker would routinely park in spaces next to the wooded area.

One day, many years ago, I left work at 4:45 p.m. (daylight savings time), and I noticed an old "Junker" car was parked next to the woods. I waited until both female workers left before leaving. The next morning I said to our secretary, "you better be careful where you park." She replied, "I'll park where ever I want." (Oh brother!)

At lunchtime I went to the Greenbrook Police Department and explained the situation. They said the police could not "stake out" the parking lot, but to call them if I saw the strange car there again and they would have a patrol car there as soon as possible.

I called home and explained the situation to Bonnie and asked her if she would "stake out" the parking lot from 4:30 to 5:15 p.m. She replied, "Yes, of course." That night… no "Junker." Second night… no "Junker." Third night, the "Junker" appeared again next to the woods at 4:50 pm. Bonnie got out of her locked car (far away, yet visible to the woods and called me from a pay phone (before cell phones) in the hospital. I told her to stay in the building until I got there.

I called the police and within five minutes two patrol cars arrived with flashing lights, and parked in front and behind the "Junker." About ten minutes later one patrol car drove over to us (Bonnie and I were standing next to the administrative entrance observing). The officer said that the driver was "crazy Tom" (his nickname) and that he worked at the diner down the road. The police told him not to park there anymore and let him go.

Bonnie and I asked the officer to talk to the two women (standing close to us at this point). He did. The situation was remedied as the two women parked close to the administrative building thereafter.

Back goes <u>Box 2227</u> with a twist of the key and we move on.

<u>BOX 7871</u>

Our creator makes a mistake every time a mentally challenged person is conceived. Need we compound this error by endangering these innocent individuals, later in life, by negligence in the Greenbrook, NJ Hospital for mentally challenged individuals?

To make a long story short, I found myself working in the basement (records section) of the Greenbrook Hospital for two days. On the second day in the basement I became fully aware that sheetrock, wooden walls, pallets and paper records on the floor were decayed and black. This was due to water seepage from the foundation. Water is necessary to promulgate mold (toxic and non-toxic), and the very large room where I was working was highly contaminated.

The contamination caused many problems. For one, toxic mold spores in the air were being circulated throughout the multi-floor hospital building via the air conditioning system--the system drew air, in part, from the basement.

At this time I turned to the "Serenity Prayer" for guidance:

"God grant me the serenity to accept the things I cannot change;

Courage to change the things I can; and the wisdom to know the difference."

I called the Commissioner of NJ Department of Health and reported the condition. The hospital administrator immediately applied for retirement -- he was afraid of losing his pension.

To make another segment of this story short, it took $500,000-$750,000 to remove the mold contamination. Workers wore protective gear similar in appearance to gear worn by men who walked on the moon. I accessed the sealed-off basement, again, (after mid-point in the remediation process) for more photos of the construction process for contingent leverage.

Low and behold, the new director of Human Services Auditing appeared at the Greenbrook audit office. We talked about 1/2 hour and I concluded that we should audit all patient charts for those who died in the past ten years and determine how many died of respiratory disease (and those currently with respiratory disorders). The director concluded his conversation by stating, "If this weren't government and you did not belong to the union, I'd fire you!" I replied, "what about the three hundred residents, and staff?..." I further stated, "I'm sure you will find a way to rid me of you."

The new director of auditing then, (after my several years of administrative work in the Greenbrook office) placed me once again in the field as an auditor. Initially, I was assigned close to home. Within six months I was driving from Easton, PA to county seats in northern New Jersey. Driving time had an adverse effect -- it wore on me.

As a result, Bonnie would drive me to work and pick me up at 5:00 p.m. After driving about three weeks to a northern New Jersey audit site, Bonnie dropped me off one morning and proceeded home. About ten minutes from the audit site, on a winding road, Bonnie fell asleep behind the wheel, ran off the road, and hit a large oak tree. The air bag saved her life. The car was totaled.

My next audit, (I was driving again after Bonnie's car accident), took me from Easton, PA, (home) to near the George Washington bridge and back daily. The drive took me two and one-half hours each way (25 hours a week plus work time) for over one month. The director of Human services auditing was not stupid…just vicious. I was almost killed and still, until today, have frequent nightmares about the driving situation. So I was forced into early retirement. This was, however a blessing in disguise. Now I was able to spend a great deal of time with Bonnie up until her death.

As a passing thought, my working with the NJ Department of Human Services has afforded me to work with various types of individuals:

> The super good
>> The good
>>> The bad and
>>>> The ugly.

Back goes <u>Box 7871</u> with a twist of the key and we move on.

BOX 0508

This text relates, in part, to gifts we made to personnel at the Greenbrook Hospital and my audit office. Bonnie and I would give "direct gifts" to those in need and those who deserve, in our opinion, worthy recognition. The gifts were fully discussed between Bonnie and I, beforehand in terms of content, amount, timing and the necessary sacrifices we would have to make in order to give them.

One such gift was twenty "Raggedy Ann" dolls, (valued at about $50 each and purchased at "7-11" for $19.95 each). The dolls were given to hospital personnel with children of appropriate ages and two black community churches. The manager of hospital recreation made the distribution.

Susan (audit secretary) received as a retirement gift from Bonnie and I, a fully paid weekend at a revolutionary war era bed and breakfast in New Hope, NJ.

Alice (audit secretary) received an undisclosed amount of cash anonymously by mail, one Christmas from us. Alice invited us over for dinner in January. She lived with her daughters and grandchildren in a very poor black section of Plainfield, NJ.

Upon entering the apartment we saw a new wide-screen television and everyone was watching a children's program. Bonnie and I were both annoyed at first; we thought the money would go to food and clothing. As the night progressed, however, Bonnie and I realized how valuable a television was to the family: learning, news, specials, sports, entertainment, history, etc. As we left that evening it was clear to us that Alice made an excellent decision for use of her cash gift. Imagine not having a television as a child or adult now a days.

Stephanie (audit secretary) received a check for thousands of dollars to aid in solving a severe family cash flow problem:

Stephanie and Frank had two children in college at the same time and were fully leveraged in terms of credit.

Back goes <u>Box 0508</u> with a twist of the key.

I must end now, even though thoughts of Bonnie are rampant in my mind, without her in my arms, but with her always in my heart. Before we end, please consider the following, also in reference to Bonnie.

Bonnie's best friend (Susan), husband (Ken) and goddaughter (Kimberly), are of Chinese descent. Bonnie studied the Chinese language and spoke some Chinese. At this point, let us look at some Chinese proverbs as a tribute to Bonnie's interest in the Chinese "way of thought."

- **Husband sings a song, wife sings along.**
- **It's a mistake to make a mistake and not correct it.**
- **Fear no mistake and not correct it.**
- **If you believe everything you read, then you better not read.**
- **Be careful about what you say - you don't know who is listening.**
- **If you want to see farther, you have to go higher.**
- **Our dreams reflect our mind.**
- **A great river is the result of many drops.**
- **Love me, love my dog.**
- **Do not swallow your food without chewing, and do not speak without thinking.**
- **The skilled commander will lead an army of skilled soldiers.**
- **The best wood is found in harsh climates.**

- Listen to both sides and be enlightened; listen to one side and be deceived.
- A tree may grow tall, but its leaves still fall back down to the roots.
- Be ashamed for not learning, rather than for not knowing.
- No clouds, no rain; no rules, no gain.
- Spoil your child, harm your child; spoil your wife, harm yourself.
- With ambition, age matters not.
- Those who are taken advantage of become wiser for it.
- Xue ru ni shui xing shou, bu jin z etui.

LETTER FROM BONNIE'S GOD DAUGHTER

Dear Gian Ma, Bonnie, God mom, whatever I called you through the years,

I can't truly express what I'm feeling. I couldn't believe it when I heard the news of your passing. Just a week ago I thought you were fine, and you were fretting (as a mother would) about me moving to the other side of the world. I apologize to everyone here today that I could not be with you all, especially to my godfather Chris.

I know I couldn't have asked for more when it came to a godmother. My mother chose her because of their friendship that had blossomed over the mutual love of St. Bernard's. Bonnie took me to countless movies where I was allowed to eat as much candy as I wanted (sorry, godmother, and Chris, for ratting you out to my mom today), dog shows, that one train show, and was there for whichever graduations, concerts, birthdays, and recitals she could make it to.

My godmother helped me through one of the hardest days of my life-when my dog was seizing and I was left alone at home - she came to my house and together along with my godfather, we saved my dogs life. I believe wholeheartedly that day helped me define who I was - that I could do the seemingly impossible as long as I had help and support of those who love me. Thank you for that.

I will miss you for all the cheeky comments you would have made about any boyfriend I might have, on my wedding day, when I have my first child, and countless memories that will be made. You were taken away too soon from us, and I hope that wherever you are that you are at peace. I love you.

Kimberly

Another part of Bonnie's life was her love of poetry, even though she wrote none to her credit; she loved those whose talents warmed her heart. Attached are the four poems to read, ponder and perhaps give a "poetic justice" to my memories of Bonnie.

Taken from: "The American Poetry Anthology" Vol. 1, Number 2, Summer 1982. Edited, with introduction, index and biographical sketches by John Frost and the staff of the American Poetry Association. The American Poetry Association, Santa Cruz, California, 1982.

<u>BEFORE YOU</u>

I was locked within myself.

I existed only in part;

the man I was meant to be

needed only the touch of you

to create the whole of me.

Your touch was the key

that opened the door

and brought light to my world;

there was only darkness before.

You set me free.

Shoulders that once were bent

from a to heavy weight

now stand tall, proud, and straight,

reaching toward the sun.

I am someone.

You loved me.

Marilyn Owens

<u>LETTING GO</u>

Love doesn't always mean being together

Sometimes love is a test

Not sharing and caring someone

But finding out if we can love someone

     enough to let them go

Parting as friends

Not enemies

Remembering the good times

The walks in the rain

And sharing the pains of life

Climbing the hills to watch the sunsets

Picking each other up at the end of a

     new beginning apart

And never ever forgetting no matter what

     lies ahead and memories will

     get us through

Lori Berteau

TIME'S UNFOLDING

Lights of my life

Song of my soul

You come to me

With all the joys of spring

Giving me love's sweet melody

While down the path of life I wander.

Where is the sadness now

That filled my heart with despair?

Gone with the snow melted by the sunshine

Bringing warmth and budding new growth.

Light of my life

Song of my soul

The depths of beauty time imparts

To know, at last to realize

Eternal blessing are indeed from One

Who opens minds and hearts to live alone.

Vivian N. Pease

LAST LOVE

I wish you the best
Of luck you see.
For you'll never know
How much you meant to me.

We once were together
But now we're apart.
So keep this memory
Close to your heart.

I told you I loved you,
I meant what I said
I will always love you,
It wasn't just in my head.

I could lean on you then,
I wish I could now,
For the memories I have
Are tearing me down.

I think of how you
Once were mine,
How everything was just fine.
You don't know when here
How harsh reality can be,

Especially when I'm alone with me.

Maureen Corrigan

Musical Favorites

AS A COUPLE...*The National Anthem*

Bonnie...

John Hiatt

Little Feat

Rock

Chris...

The Association (Cherish)

Celtic

Beethoven (All #'s)

CONCLUSION OF
CHAPTER

Time, certainly not lack of memories of Bonnie, has run out for now. Hopefully, opening a few "memory boxes" will give additional "light" about her to both those who met her only once or so, and those who knew of her kindness. Of course, saying how she gave on a day-to-day basis is not practical; but, believe me, she was always there to give whatever way she could. We were a perfect "match" in terms of giving, sharing, appreciating, having fun, and of course, loving one another until death did us part and thereafter.

Bonnie hasn't died, she just shed her body and joined all those faithfully departed in heaven. "Death" has always been the hardest part of life to me since a child to the present. Bonnie's passing is no exception. Naively, I never gave death a thought, nor that it would happen to Bonnie.

Bonnie's passing, however, opened many happy doors that otherwise may never have been opened. I had a "calling" and joined organizations where my talents would be highly productive and appreciated.

The work I now do is directed to the following:

"If we can't turn the world around we can at least bolster the victims."

-Liz Carpenter

CHAPTER IX

CHRISTOPHER'S EMAILS:

COUSINS

FORWARD

All my cousins, in my opinion, have "shunned" me for over forty years. Only a few times was I invited to family gatherings – usually as a conduit to drive my mother. Once my mother passed, everything came to an abrupt halt. My first and second wives were never given an amicable healthy inclusion in family affairs over the years. Only my aunt was good-natured to us on occasion, except, perhaps her 90th birthday party where neither Bonnie nor I were invited to. Be that as it may, I have made an earnest attempt to come to reconciliation with one cousin that is addressed in this chapter by a series of actual emails between us. The Christmas letter and first email back to me portray these two cousins as living a life style where everything is "rosey." As you may find in this chapter, I made a sincere effort to extend my feelings, emotions, and in the end, anger for even trying...

HAPPY NEW YEAR'S LETTER:

(FROM A COUSIN)

We tried but not did succeed in getting a Christmas letter out this year. We wish you and your family a wonderful 2013 with great health, happiness and good fortune throughout the year. 2012 was a good year for the McCarthy's: We had a fun Reunion with Dave's D-2 West Point classmates in Orlando and Wilbur–by--the Sea hosted by Rodger and Kittie Smith in April which was immediately followed by a grand Reunion with my sister, May and brother in law James Harrow at Singer Island. In May we had our annual Beach Week in Nags Head with our children and grandchildren. Karen and Ted celebrated their 25th wedding anniversary at Smithfield Station Inn in July – a gift from their children! We all joined the happy couple for brunch.

In September we spent two weeks in Ireland with Fred – his 50th birthday gift. He enjoyed driving on the Irish roads – obviously he likes the challenge. We had spectacular accommodations in castles and country inns, ideal weather, and a chance to meet with some Irish relatives in Kilkee and friends in Dublin. Dave turned 75 on Thanksgiving Day but was surprised with an early birthday party in October! I retired form real estate on October 31st.

Our saddest day was when we said goodbye to Jessie as she crossed over the Rainbow Bridge in October. Jessie was our 11 ½ yr. old golden retriever. Who was a wonderful, loving friend to us. Dave is in his fourth year as Treasurer of our regional Golden Retriever Rescue and has found another dog, Peanut aka PJ, to welcome into our family. She is of course a Golden and devoted to Dave – she follows him everywhere – like a parade.

Sadly Hurricane Sandy virtually destroyed Dave's sister Alice's house in Freehold, NJ. The fate of this house, in the McCarthy family for fifty years, remains to be seen.

In July we made the decision to move to Anchor Colony, a retirement community in Annapolis, MD. Our house there is almost ready. We expect to be there by February 1st.

Best Wishes for the Best Year Yet in 2013!!

Sharon and Dave

Dear Sharon & Dave,

Thanks so much for your "Happy New Year" letter, I was very pleased to receive it, it is unfortunate the last time I saw the "McCarthy's," before Pattie's passing, was at Jonathan's funeral. This situation is most unfortunate to say the least!! As a result, I am writing to you for many reasons.

I trust everyone received my disclosure after Bonnies passing – it was good to relay some facts about our private lives to so many relatives and friends. I have not dated since Bonnie's death, but, interestingly enough, I have regained contact with one of my high school and college girlfriends via the internet - she has a home in New York, Maine, Florida and who knows, maybe with me in Pennsylvania.

Presently my time is largely spent donating to "GIVE BACKS." Namely, in my associations with The Police Athletic League, Kiwanis, Catholic Charities and the Salvation Army in Easton. Man, I am having so much fun in doing so. With my accounting background and humanistic view on life, I am in great demand. I am really happy to be so active in helping the unfortunate and myself.

Now, on the other hand, I have also found several hobbies. One is model railroading. I joined a club in Bethlehem that has two tremendous layouts and found "working–on–the–railroad" very pleasurable and relaxing. Another hobby is involvement with sports cars – you may have seen my "Z-4" at Pattie's funeral. I had a corvette stingray in high school and wanted to renew my "sporty image" again. Many of my friends say I am living my second childhood – they are probably right.

Because of our lack of communication over the years, I do not know if Sue or Karen have daughters. The reason I ask goes way back in time. Shortly before Pop Jake died he left me his two personal items in the world – Sapphire and diamond cufflinks and a large biblical painting. I turned the cufflinks into a woman's necklace for my first wife, Chandise. I regained the necklace shortly after our divorce. Bonnie also wore it. At this point in time, I believe the necklace should go to a female (blood relative) who will in turn pass it down to their daughter and maintain the lineage in the future amongst female descendants. Please let me know if my intent with the necklace is possible. As for the painting, I have naturally kept it as a memory of the family as I once knew it and cherished it the most.

At Pattie's funeral dinner, Alice indicated to me that the two of you are quite the world travelers. How about a trip to my house? I still live in the same house as Bonnie and I did in Easton and have ample room (seven bedrooms). It would be great to show you the sites and meet some of my friends – one of which was a Captain in the Navel Reserves. Dave, bear in mind that West Point is under a two hour drive. Also Dave, I recently sent in my contribution to the West Point Association of Graduates. The Army credit card I showed you after Pattie's viewing, was a Bank of America Visa Card and can be processed by calling Customer Service at 1-800-421-2110.

May I end my email with a quote from a "former" accountant:

"The truism of responsibility is accountability."

Bye for now,

Chris

EMAIL – II   Sun, Mar. 3, 2013 at 11:03 AM

Hi Chris,

Thank you for your email – I am so glad you have found such a great place to live and that you are enjoying your life there. You have managed to put together a great life for yourself. One thing on my Bucket List is to visit Lehigh U, where my father and brother went. So when we do get that way, we will let you know!

I spoke to both Karen and Sue about the necklace you have. They both, and I agree, feel that Pop would be happiest to have Christina now have the necklace. She is your niece and so much closer to you than our daughters are. Rather than it be a McCarthy heirloom, it could now be a Paltz heirloom. I appreciate your offer.

Good luck with your high school/ College friend. She sounds interesting and well housed!

Best to you…..Sharon

EMAIL – III   Sun, Mar 3, 2013 at 12:52 PM

To: Sharon

Hi again,

The only reservation I have in giving it to Christina is that she has about thirty thousand (wholesale) of jewelry from my mother (mostly from Aunt Rebecca). I will further deliberate about the necklace and will probably leave it as a codicil to my will.

Lehigh U is about twenty minutes from my house. Maybe I will see you before the next funeral, certainly not a wedding…

   Chris

EMAIL – IV   Tue, Mar 5, 2013 at 10:50 AM

Dear Sharon and Dave,

Just one last email and I will put this to rest. The main reason I want to pass the necklace on to one of your daughters (or some kind of arraignment) is to the one(s) who served in the armed services. This is most important to me, like Dave, that they served our country as part of their lives – I failed to state this in my last email. To be quite frank about this matter, I do not think Christina would appreciate the necklace. The decision is mine to make.

If you had reservations about staying at my home, you could have always have stayed at a hotel.

It is most disheartening to never have been invited to any of my cousin's children's weddings (McCarthy's). For example, more resonantly, Grace's wedding. I am sure you would not like this situation if it were you.

I too am serving our country as an active participant in the Salvation Army, amongst the other organizations I am affiliated with.

Now, it is time to formally say goodbye to the McCarthy's….   Chris

Chris,

I was very surprised and upset by your last email. Sharon and I (and our children) did nothing to deserve your harsh turnabout with respect to us and our family.

We were glad to hear from you in response to the letter we sent earlier this year that summarized our 2012 and let our extended family and closest friends know our plans to move to a retirement community. This was a major change for us and would entail a great deal of thought and effort. We continue to be in the midst of getting things completed both at our new home and also at the house that we will shortly be putting on the market.

We were glad to hear from you and were a little taken back by your generosity in thinking of us, our girls, etc. as the beneficiary of the necklace you had made from heirloom jewelry that had belonged to Pop. Growing up, no one was closer to Pop in our family than me and, in fact, we continued throughout my years at West Point. I remember clearly how proud Nanny and Pop were to attend my graduation. This made your offer so much more meaningful to me.

Sharon and I discussed the matter and, independently, both thought of Christina. We understood your rationale for keeping the jewelry in the "bloodline" but thought it appropriate for us to share with you our thoughts. Sharon also discussed the matter with our daughters, Karen and Sue, and they were of the same opinion. You should not take our opinions as a rejection of your preference. It is your property and obviously you have more information with respect to Christina and the family heirlooms she has inherited than we do. We have no knowledge about that or about any inheritance from Aunt Rebecca.

I do not see any reason for you to cut yourself off from all the McCarthy's. I also don't understand your comments regarding weddings. The weddings of our children were small and we were not able to invite our first cousins on either side of the family. No one should have felt slighted. Your comment about Grace's wedding is particularly confusing. The only Grace in the family is Alberta and Richard's daughter. She has never been married.

In closing, let's see what we can work out that is amendable to all concerned.

Dave

Dave,

You must agree that I have been slighted by the family – there is no question about this fact. There are many things to be considered in respect to us having a meeting of the minds…let's begin.

Most importantly is Nanny and Pop. Some of my earliest recollections begin in Montclair. I remember the family Christmas dinners (Thanksgiving, too) we had, as if they were yesterday. The manger in the window, the Christmas trees with lights on them and remembrances of Darlene's migraines. These were the days when Nanny and Pop lived on the third floor. They were most fond of you, especially when you were recommended and attended West Point. I was very young then. I also remember trips to West Point to visit you. You are most correct of how proud they were of you at your graduation. It was when the hats were in the air that tears were running down from Nanny's eyes – this was quite a sight to have taken in, all at once.

When I grew older I lived for a period of time with Nanny and Pop in New York City while attending college. It was then when I spent a great deal of time with Pop e.g., in the park – Pop would often listen to the Yankees while I studied. As time progressed Pop's health failed. This is when I was "feeding" oxygen to him while studying for finals. Then, he shortly passed away at my mothers and Nanny thereafter. I sincerely think it was a tie between you and me for his favorite; however, he truly loved his entire family, this was his nature.

If we look back to the memories of Nanny and Pop they can provide a "common ground" for us to rebuild a more encompassing family rather than maintain it as a stagnate one.

About ten years ago a former friend and co-worker of mine would go to West Point every year for a football game – his son was a graduate of the academy, of Philippine background and was a Catholic. We always made it a point to go early and watch the Cadet Parade prior to the game and visit the Catholic Church. Bonnie and I also spent our wedding night, in a suite, at the Thayor Hotel in West Point – the academy and hotel was that important and enjoyable to us (the hotel's food was outstanding, too). As a passing thought, before we move on, remember your sports car that you owned. At the time, it was said you had a choice between getting married or the car. We would kid you to keep the car. In retrospect, I think Sharon will laugh at this now but was not happy with the comment at the time! It is not too late to get a sports car now (as a second car), like me, and regain a sporty life style again.

As I reflect further on the necklace, I certainly do not want to cause any controversy. Maybe a more viable idea would be to contribute it to a museum that specializes in the period that it originated from. This would enable untold thousands to appreciate it with an inscription in reference to: Jake "Pop's" Campbell and family. It should be a permanent part of an exhibit, and not be sold in the future. The agreement would have to be a steadfast one. I am most eager to determine an equitable solution, such as the one I proposed in this paragraph. I have indicated my preference in prior emails; but I also do not want to be myopic in my decision.

As to the painting Pop left me, it is considered "worthless" by the art auctioneer's in New York City. The painting needs complete restoration (at an expensive price). The painting is also in need of a frame, too. It is my hope to someday restore it.

Aunt Rebecca gave my mother numerous pieces of diamond jewelry before her passing. I saw many of the diamond pieces of jewelry. I think all, or most of it, was part of my mother's estate. Walley purchased many of the pieces when we settled my mother's estate. Upon Walley's death, Pattie received the portion Walley bought. Bruce probably has all of it in his possession and is holding them for Christina. I am really confused in this whole matter, but this is correct as to "my" understanding.

Time spans between me seeing my cousin's ranges widely and over very significant periods of time. When Bonnie passed, I was told that Darlene, Julie, Alice and Leslie were on a trip – was this so? In any case, I did not see or speak to you, Sharon, Rocco or Richard.

Flowers were, in my opinion, not a substitute for a personal or verbal contact in my time of need. The only relatives present then were my son Rob, Pattie, and Bruce. More than another four years passed without contact until Pattie's death. This whole matter becomes a complicated "mess" if you analyze the time spans. In my opinion, I was clearly slighted, to say the least, over considerable periods of time without citing specific examples. When was the last time I had seen any of your children before Pattie's funeral? Also, in respect to my family, when was the last you have seen Rob, Suzanne, Robbie and Julie? In my opinion, we have all failed as concerning relatives and are all at fault.

It is strange that I felt slighted and you would have had no concern in the matter if I did not email you. After Bonnie's death, I sent a long narrative disclosure of some of the events we shared in our marriage to, for one, my "McCarthy" cousins in hope of regaining contact with you guys. I received not a reply, except from my friends. I also sent a picture of Nanny and Heidi (St. Bernard) as a further hope of contact; but, there was also not a word in response.

Let's summarize this situation. Our families have not been in what would be considered a healthy family relationship for many decades. I attempted to extend knowledge and feelings to your family by email. Sharon's answer was elusive as to any specific time(s) in the future. I fully realize you are moving and the disruption this causes. Maybe, at this point, I can assist you in moving? I would like to extend my help (naturally, for free) in your move. My help, and maybe other help from your siblings and family, would be realistic means to regain lost time and have a great deal of fun in doing so!! Please do not dismiss the idea.

Consider the above and any other ideas you may have, as to rebuilding our family…

Chris

P.S. Bonnie and I were not invited to your mother's ninetieth birthday party – another painful fact to live with.

EMAIL – VII   Sun, Mar 17, 2013 at 3:18 PM

Dave & Sharon,

I think a statement in a former email of mine needs further clarification. If we look back to the days when our country was being settled, it was often common for settlers to help one another in providing friendship to a new family in the area. Most often, neighbors would collectively "pitch-in" by aiding in the construction of a new house and, if applicable, a barn in a farming setting. The feeling of friendship flourished within the community as new relationships were developed and old ones, amongst former settlers, were further renewed.

This concept, for all practicable purposes, is unheard of in present times.

To be more specific, in my prior email, I offered my help in your future move. I also suggested that it may be possible for our relatives to be of assistance too. Dave, I think presenting the idea to the family would be most helpful to you and all concerned.

As things develop in the moving process we are all capable of packing and unpacking boxes under your supervision. The trying choices of what to keep would be most difficult for you. A garage sale(s) would not be beyond your expectations of us. I spent the better part of ten years driving trucks (in my own business and landscaping) and am proficient in this area. I cannot lift heavy objects, but can assist in lighter ones.

Darlene may be of specific help in decorating while unpacking boxes. Leslie specifically stated at Pattie's funeral lunch, that Richard is constantly complaining he has nothing to do – he may be the most significant one in the entire process! Tiffany and Robin would have to determine how they would help. Let us not forget your children and Sharon's family too.

One of the most stressful parts of your life now, could turn into a "piece of cake." I think the concepts are worth considering and acting upon – do you?

Chris

EMAIL – VIII   Sun, Mar 17, 2013 at 5:15 PM

Chris,

We completed our move early last month and are settled and established in our new forever retirement continuing care community. Our children and older grandchildren were a big help and our former home is now ready to be put on the market. At this point we don't really need any help.

Thanks for your thoughts on how the family could have helped us but we really didn't need it.

Your conversation with Alberta regarding Grace cannot possibly be factual as she has never been married.

Dave

Christopher's final conclusion…

If all that concerns my cousins Dave and Sharon is that I know that Grace is not married; MAN, have I wasted my time and efforts.

Believe me, the rest of my cousins are even worse than Dave and Sharon. It is clear to me, that the sun has settled in the West, and will never rise again in the East, as the blackness of stagnation prevails in my "family."

<u>In all earnest I must again, and finally, say goodbye to all my cousins NOW!!!</u>

So be it.

Christopher

CHAPTER X

CHRISTOPHER'S EMAILS:

BROTHER

IN

LAW

FORWARD

My relationship amongst congregation of friends has always been very good. Unfortunately, my relationship with my sister and brother-in-law was ill fated at times, more often than not.

My sister died of lung cancer over a relatively short period of time. Before her passing I made concerted efforts to reconcile our differences before her death. I extended myself as earnestly as I know how – she accepted my forgiveness and we loved one another for the remainder of her short life.

My brother-in-law is a different story. We really did not ever try to establish a friendship or any communication between us. This condition lasted for over 40 years, as with my sister. I felt, after my sister's death, we should establish a friendlier relationship within a reasonable amount of time. Upon reading our emails, the reader should be able to formulate if my conclusion is apt.

EMAIL –BRUCE MURPHY /CHRISTINA MURPHY/CHRIS PALTZ

Thu, Mar 21, 2013

Hi Bruce,

I am writing for several reasons:

How is your health "holding" up?? The first heard of your condition was from Bonnie Steps and then in Christina's belated Christmas letter. I will address this circumstance later in this email.

I purposely set aside an issue of great importance to me, before Pattie passed away, until now. That was to make reconciliation with you. I did not attempt this until the present time because I thought it could have confused and, possibly, impede the final bonding between Pattie and myself. I sincerely hope I was correct in my thoughts and actions. It was also most imperative that I spent time with Pattie and you, in your home, before she passed away.

It is difficult to put into words the good and bad times that we experienced over the years. It is important that we discuss both, in a limited manner, to effectuate a sound reconciliation.

I think the most important matter is your military career and the fact that you donated your life to our country. This is the <u>most</u> noble contribution anyone can do – and you successfully did it! This would not have been possible without Pattie, Sam and Christina at your side – They were and are so proud of you as well as myself. The fact that you served in several wars, from in a submarine to setting up a land hospital also indicates your dedication. Let's not forget the education you gained in the service as a means to better serve our country. It is also most important, that we discuss two happy occasions that reflected upon your career's accomplishments. One was a family recognition and the other a formal Naval appreciation of your service. The family recognition was when both of our families gathered and presented you with a Mort Kunstler civil war print – "Raise the Colors and Follow Me" upon return from war. I particularly remember your mother beaming at the time. The formal Naval event was your retirement ceremony when we witnessed both a happy and sad (your leaving duty) moment at the same time. As the rifles sounded and echoed in our minds, it was a most somber moment to all those attending and praying for you.

Now, it is most difficult to discuss three painful family events in our lives. Try and bear with me. First, in part, was Sam's death. With my experiences at death dating back to my father's I could not attend his viewing at the time. This was no reflection on your family but a reality I could not face – losing someone very important in life devastates me. At Pattie's viewing I was unable to actually view her, but it was the best I could possibly have done. I was slighted by you in Pattie's funeral process when, at the Mass, you did not want me to sit with you and Christina. Further, you did not want me to attend the burial and luncheon thereafter – this was specifically implied at your home after the viewing. I accepted your rejections based on previous matters, over the years.

The second painful event, in my opinion, as also noted in my email to Pattie, was my behavior with my mother's will. I stated in her email that I was a "jerk" and was sorry for my behavior. I extend my apology to you also. I believe that there may have been some "substance vs. form" issues (Gregory vs. Helvering) as executor, but as Pattie stated, I was not in the "loop." The whole situation, at the time, was most unfortunate for all of us involved. I fully intend to put the "estate issue" to rest, unless you feel it needs further edification.

… The third issue is Patties death. I will continue to try and put it into perspective and the mourning process as an acceptable part of life. Please note, just weeks ago, one of my best friend's father died. I also continue not to view the body while paying my respects to the family. The family respected my wishes as I explained my situation and were happy I came to see the family (in the hallway) even though I did not witness the body. I feel that, in recent years, my seeing the family is best without seeing the body – this approach is better than when I rejected the entire viewing process, as when Sam died. The new path is most effective in my case of handling the funeral process.

Bruce if it is possible, I would like to make amends with you (and Christina) as to the past and hopefully build a bondage between our families that can exist for the remainder of our lives. This is hard to ask for, but it would be the healthiest step we can make as a united family.

On another positive note, have you framed the limited edition print I gave you – it is quite unusual to have a piece of art actually signed by Major Doolittle, too. Would it look nice in your den? or downstairs? Actually, I am giving away most of my collection of limited edition art. I have a Mort Kunstler civil war print called "The Glorious Fourth" when Ulysses S. Grant is riding on a horse into Vicksburg and naval ships are in the background. I also have other Naval prints I think you would appreciate in your home, as a gift.

Recently, I have replaced my American Flag on the outside of my house with a new one. Below the new American flag I also have another new flag – a Naval Jack. It is a smaller flag with a dark blue background and white stars. It was flown, in the past, to designate when a naval ship or boat was in port. The two complement each other extremely well as I am sure you are aware.

As a final consideration, my invitation for you to visit and stay at my home, is still open as I mentioned in recent phone calls. There are numerous activities to do in the area, as well as day trips. For example, there is a museum called "America on Wheels" that has auto exhibits from the first autos and trucks to the present – it is very interesting. Nancy and Mike live only about 10 minutes away. Possibly, lunch with Francine (a former Captain in the Nursing Corps), which you met at the luncheon after Bonnie's burial. In addition, near Francine's home, is the Rutgers Art Museum (a large permanent Russian Exhibit as well as a significant American Collection of Art) – a nice afternoon. There is a Casino twenty minutes from my home if you are so interested or even for just a visit. The Battle Ship New Jersey is in Camden, NJ and is under a two hour drive. West Point is also under a two hour trip. Historic Philadelphia is also nearby. In addition, I have been thinking of having my friends who served in the armed services over for a mid-afternoon lunch/dinner if you come. As noted below, are those to be invited:

You, Paul, Raymond, Joe, Walt (Police), Bernie, Cassie, Tom, Don.

There are also numerous collegiate sports in the area – Lafayette, Lehigh U., Seton Hall (about 40 minutes away) and Rutgers. At West Point, maybe fencing would be going on? There are also many very good (reasonably priced) restaurants in the area. If you are into "birding" there are many great places to observe them – migrating birds are really exciting! The Statue of Liberty is closed; but I think Ellis Island is open. A ride on the Staten Island Ferry is always a great experience. Finally, a visit to your family grave site is about one half an hour away.

Naturally, Christina and Jane are <u>always most welcome</u> too!! I assume Christina may have to work?? Maybe vacation time would permit a visit?

With highest regards…..

Chris

EMAIL- UNION JACK AND COMMENTS

Sat, Apr 20, 2013

Hi Chris,

I received the flag and I will use it, thank you.

I've been at a loss as to how to respond to your note about Pattie's funeral. I was quite surprised by your comments.

In no way did I intentionally refuse to allow you to join the family at the mass.

I know that you are very uncomfortable with funerals and quite frankly I was surprised to see you come at all. If you stayed away I would have been ok with that and accepted your situation. Since you did come I rather unconsciously decided to give you your space and let you get as closely involved, as you felt comfortable.

I did not specifically invite you to join Christina and I for that reason. Also you have to remember, you have been distant from our family in so many ways for several years and it has been uncomfortable for me to have you rejoin it at such a peak moment as Patties funeral and to regard you as if it we have been physically and emotionally close continuously over the years.

Several months ago I told you that I thought I would be able to get up your way in the spring. At this point, I don't know when or if that will happen and it is not related to the above issues. My cardiac rehab continues to the beginning of May and I'm starting a theology course in June. I do want to get up to visit Pattie's and Sam's gravesite, but it will be a quick trip. A monument that I recently purchased has been installed and I haven't seen it yet. Sally does not do well with her "Grand-daddy" away and now that I am feeling stronger, there is a lot I want to get done around my house.

Take Care,

Bruce

EMAIL - NAVY JACK AND YOUR VISIT?

Mon, Apr 22, 2013

Hi Bruce,

I was very happy to receive your email! I am also happy you received the "Navy Jack" I sent you. As you know the Navy Jack has been replaced by the words "Do Not Tread on Me." If you look at the original flag, the blue and white stars are identical to the blue and white stars section of the American Flag – coincidental? In my "Victory at Sea" disks, one episode shows five sailors waving five Navy Jacks with what appears to have forty eight stars on each flag. I am curious about this. I do know the flag was flown when a ship or boat was in port.

I do understand your thoughts on Pattie's funeral and agree with you. Thank you for your understanding at the time.

I am not sure from your email if you are coming for a visit or not? I certainly hope you do! Let me know of your plans when they are more apparent. I do know we would have lots of fun and regain lost time, also.

With Highest Regards,

Chris

EMAIL– A VISIT TO THE USS INTREPID, TOO?

Fri, Apr 26, 2013

Hi Bruce,

I really hope you come for a visit! I forgot to mention is a visit to the USS INTREPID SEA, AIR AND SPACE MUSEUM in New York City. New additions, are the USS GROWLER submarine and a Concorde Jet (without wings) – both of which you can tour inside. The museum is "loaded" with history and almost 30 aircraft on display. If you have not been there recently the trip is most worthwhile.

As I mentioned in my previous email there are numerous things to do in the area which might interest you – I think we could both use a nice diversion in our lives, of which would be really be fun and relaxing to us.

With Highest Regards,

Chris

There has been no further contact between Bruce and I, except his one email dated April 20, 2013 through September 30, 2014.

Christopher's Personal Conclusion...

My only brother-in-law was puzzled by the first email I sent to him. As noted in the emails I presented, we had our differences over the years. My attempt at a reconciliation proved to be fruitless. It appears the blackness of stagnation prevails, and I wasted my time and efforts in starting a friendship with Bruce. I have no qualms with Bruce but must say Bon Voyage and wish him well – I have finished my attempts at a formative, prospective, friendship.

So be it.

Christopher

CHAPTER XI

PLIGHT
TO
AMERICA

TRANSPORTATION

Photo Source: (Top) File: Air.india.b747-400.onground.arp.jpg (Bottom) File:Air_India_2.jpg

EDUCATION

PRINCETON   HARVARD

YALE   PENN

CORNELL   DARTMOUTH

COLUMBIA   BROWN

TRANSPORTATION

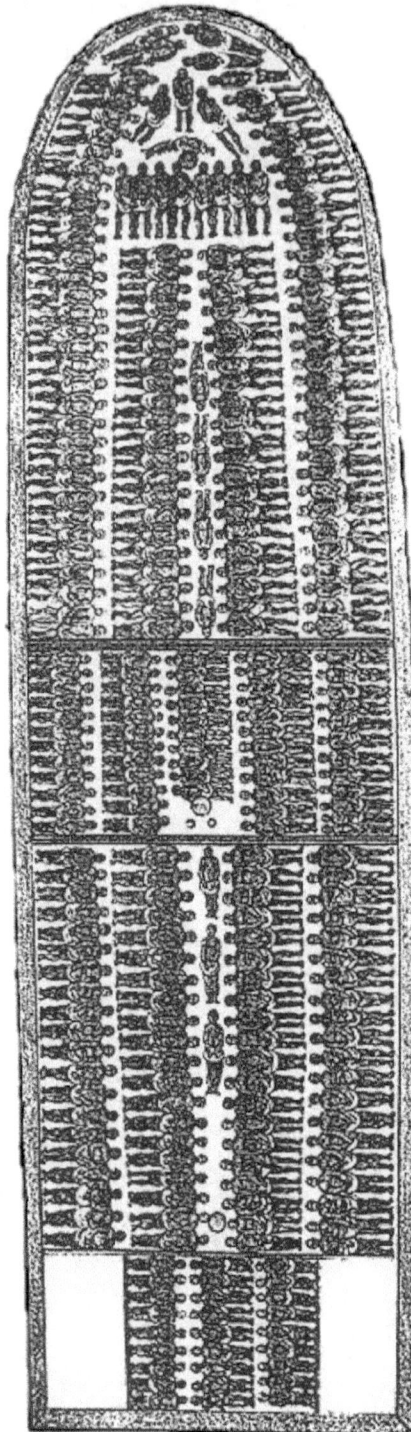

AFRICAN SLAVE SHIP

Photo Source: *Library of Congress*

EDUCATION

Photo Source: "THE HISTORY OF AMERICAN GRAFFITI" by Roger Gastman & Caleb Neelon. February 05, 2011.

BLIND
INJUSTICE

BLIND
INJUSTICE

Photo Source: Lady Justice; Roman goddess of justice.

LINDA MY LOVE...

CHAPTER XII

Songs of the Soul

Cherish

Sung by Association
Lyrics by Terry Kirkman, 1966

Cherish is the word I describe

Of the feeling that I have hiding here for you inside

You don't know how many times I've wished that I had told you

You don't know how many times I've wished that I could hold you

You don't know how many times I've wished that I could mold you

Into someone who could cherish me as much as I cherish you

Cherish is the word that more than applies

To the hope in my heart each time I realize

That I am not gonna be the one to share your dreams

That I am not gonna be the one to share your schemes

That I am not gonna be the one to share what seems to be

The life that you could cherish as much as I do yours

Oh, I'm beginning to think that man has never found

The words that could make you want me

That have the right amount of letters, just the right sound

That could make you hear, make you see

That you are driving me out of my mind

Oh, I could say I need you, but then you'd realize

That I want you, just like a thousand other guys

Who'd say they loved you with all the rest of their lives

When all they wanted was to touch your face your hands
And gaze into your eyes

Cherish is the word I use to describe

Of the feeling that I have hiding here for you inside

You don't know how many times I've wished that I had told you

You don't know how many times I've wished that I could hold you

You don't know how many times I've wished that I could mold you

Into someone who could cherish me as much as I cherish you

And I do cherish you

And I do cherish you

Cherish is the word

LINDA... MY LOVE

Why was it, while so young, we saw love in one another ???

Was it was because we were reckless at the time, or that the seeds of the future were lain???

I can only imagine, as I think back, at the beauty you beheld...

Is it all possible there was a seed in our souls that would not propagate for another forty year cycle

I can only think, that as impossible as it may be, such a seed was planted, in our hearts so long ago..

Can you remember riding in my corvette, as reckless as we were... leaving the "Big Apple" after a night of disco and heavy drinking, only to have you vomit in my lap, as we passed through the Lincoln Tunnel on route to your your home... remember the next morning when you went out to clean it up ?

Can you remember the night, when we were not so reckless at 2:00am
and we waded in the fountain at the Lincoln Center in the "Big Apple"
our feet and legs were all so wet as the water spout up around us...
was it possible that the seeds of a future love were cast???
The guard of the complex, while watching us,
had a smile on his face, as he wondered
over to us, and said "I am so
glade this fountain
has a purpose...

We were young and perhaps so reckless, at the time... that we did not know what we were dealing with at the moment. We did not know that our intimacy was so precious, serious, enjoyable and religious. How could we, at the time we were only eighteen/ nineteen. It is almost impossible for couples so young to find love without trial or error, in search of a true love that will last for our lifetime on this planet!!

Should we look at our at our reckless relationships with remorse or part of growing up???

Can you remember when, at the age of eighteen or nineteen, we were so easily attracted...
Is it possible that you remember me paying to have your initials embroiled on
shirts sleeves??? Was this a "branding," of a lasting love in our hearts???
I can only imagine, as impossible as it may seem, I was to
brand your heart again another day...
Your initials while only three, spelled
a four letter word called LOVE,
Is it possible that you
to saw it that
way???

The

word thanksgiving

has many connotations, but lets

look at just one. My heart has been over

come by want, not that of food, but want of seeing

you. I am so starved for a meal of looking into your eyes,

touching your hands and whispering in your ear, how much I truly love you.

I remember so clearly, as we dinned at the "tavern on the Green," one enchanted

evening, and our picture was taken by their photographer. We were so young, so carefree, a time

without want. We had each other, and like a drop of wine, our love was the gift of a powerful waterfall.

Alas,

It is the Holiday

season past, when I remember

so clearly when you called me at Thanks-

giving to wish me a happy "Easter," yes "Easter" on

my answering machine. The message was quite clear, as tears

ran down my cheeks as I knew I was in your thoughts - this elated me beyond

belief. I envisioned your beauty as only my memories could. Alas, it is Thanksgiving

present and not a word from you. SALT-WATER tears rain down my face into an open wound

that hurt so profusely that it was as if my heart was stung by a thousand killer wasps!!! Pain is the word.

It

is only fair to me,

that you realize what you have

done, in part, to me. When you captured

my heart you were able to crystallize my fragile mind.

My thoughts and memories were to chime when the feelings

and emotions were subject to the breezes and storms of my life.

How can it be that when my mind does chime I see a crystal clear image of you with

your hair blowing in the wind, a look of excitement in your eyes and a smile that would have

warmed our troops at Valley Forge. Over the years the crystals you implanted in my mind would only

flicker when my memories of you were electrified by the turning of a switch. Will the prisms of my life lie dormant?

GOD

Why couldn't our relationship

lasted forever? In all do course, we parted our ways,

as you dated others. Upon departmentation I was devastated and turned

to my drug of choice -- 175,000 pints of Budweiser over a considerable number of years. Yet,

even after several detox's and a successful Rehab, I kicked the alcohol addiction 23 years ago. Man, it is like being

born again except there is a hollowness as found in a drained coconut. Was I to be re-born again by pecking on my outer shell or perhaps

be a still born? I am in such pain... pain that may never be resolved... pain that will not allow me to fully love again.

Pain in knowing that I have not been the one to share your schemes, not to be the one

to share your dreams. Pain in not to be the one to share your beauty!!

To

be honest,

are we acting as

responsible adults? I am telling

you my innermost feelings in hopes of

regaining the impossible. You are in turn, trying

to crush my feelings by silence and casting my feelings of love into

the darkness and stagnation of eternity.

Linda,

touch my heart in any way

you wish and you will see the happiest person

in the world -- try it, and see!

O Linda, O Linda, O Linda

My love,

Christopher

Songs of the Soul

"OFF THE GROUND"

Written and Sung by Paul McCarthney, 1993

THERE MUST HAVE BEEN A LOT OF HEARTACHE

FOR YOU TO SINK SO LOW.

YOU MUST HAVE HAD A TON OF PRESSURE,

ONLY ANSWER IF THE ANSWER'S NO.

I NEED LOVING, YOU NEED LOVING TOO.

DOESN'T TAKE A LOT TO GET OFF THE GROUND.

THERE MUST HAVE BEEN A LOT OF MAGIC

WHEN THE WORLD WAS BORN.

LET ME BE THE ONE YOU WISH FOR,

ONE YOU CALL FOR, WHEN YOU'RE ALL ALONE, MM-MM.

I NEED LOVING, YOU NEED LOVING TOO.

WOULDN'T TAKE A LOT TO GET OFF THE GROUND.

OFF THE GROUND, LA-LA-LA-LA-LA-LA
OFF THE GROUND, LA-LA-LA-LA-LA-LA
FLY AROUND, LA-LA-LA-LA-LA-LA
FLY AROUND, LA-LA-LA-LA-LA-LA.
HEAR THE SOUND, HEAR THE SOUND,
OFF THE GROUND, LA-LA-LA-LA-LA-LA
OFF THE GROUND, LA-LA-LA-LA-LA-LA.

OH.

THOUGH IT TAKES A LOT OF POWER

TO MAKE A BIG TREE GROW,

IT DOESN'T NEED A POT OF KNOWLEDGE,

*FOR A SEED KNOWS WHAT A SEED MUST
KNOW, MM-MM.*

YOU NEED LOVING, (you need loving)

I NEED LOVIN TOO. (I need loving too)

DOESN'T TAKE A LOT TO GET OFF THE GROUND.

*OFF THE GROUND, LA-LA-LA-LA-LA-LA
OFF THE GROUND, LA-LA-LA-LA-LA-LA
FLY AROUND, LA-LA-LA-LA-LA-LA
FLY AROUND, LA-LA-LA-LA-LA-LA.
HEAR THE SOUND, HEAR THE SOUND,
OFF THE GROUND, LA-LA-LA-LA-LA-LA
OFF THE GROUND, LA-LA-LA-LA-LA-LA.*

*HEAR THE SOUND, HEAR THE SOUND,
OFF THE GROUND, LA-LA-LA-LA-LA-LA
OFF THE GROUND, LA-LA-LA-LA-LA-LA.*

YEAH, YEAH, OFF THE GROUND.

"Hours Before the Mid-Night Drag"

Photo Source: Lincoln Center

THE END
of
LINDA MY LOVE
CHAPTER

CHAPTER XIII

PREFERANCE

The proposed "Case Study: Military Strategy" combines the collective resources of many NATO countries to form a "shield" by utilizing military maneuvers in NATO countries that boarder Russia. Naval strategy also exhibits an imperative dimension to the complete plan. While the theater of events change in reality, the reader of the plan will be asked to make "Military Strategy" decisions at the conclusion of the proposed plan.

One must ask, and rightfully so, is it better to deal with Russian aggression <u>now</u>, while the ball is still in NATO's "court?" It has often been commented, by individuals in authority, that NATO lacks meaningful leadership, even when human life and national sovereignty are at risk!!! This statement, in my opinon, is true and must be acted upon immediately. There is no time to hold extensive deliberations, economic sanctions or to take the position of "lets wait and see what happens" attitude.

<u>It is clear to me, that a new individual must be given full command and responsibility of the proposed "Military Stratgey" before Ukraine becomes a deadly force to be reconciled with.</u>

NATO: North Atlantic Treaty Organization

An organization of 28 member countries across North America and Europe, which constitutes a system of collective defense whereby its member countries agree to mutual defense in response to an attack by any external party. It is important to note that any aggressive action, by Russia, against the Ukraine, **while not a NATO member**, could lead to future military action against NATO member countries and non-NATO independant nations.

CASE STUDY:

MILITARY STRATEGY
(UKRAINE CONFLICT)

This case study concerns NATO, Russian and the Ukraine conflict and potential war. First and formost, this entire proposal is done with the consent of NATO.

NATO nations will be engaged in strategic exercises with full knowledge by the Russians. The proposal will indicate to the Russians that the actions, by NATO countries, are **non-aggressive** and only an exercise in **"military systems and procedures."**

The NATO maneuvers in this case study are designed such that there will be no human injury or death. Further, there will be no movement of land troops and/or military land assets (e.g. tanks).

The NATO plan calls for:

1. Two NATO aircraft carrier formations.
2. Use of B-52 and B1-B supersonic aircraft bombers.
3. "ICBM" is an abreviation for "Intercontinental Ballistic Missile." Utilization of <u>Peaceful</u> ICBM's (non-nuclear war-heads) will be launched from NATO submarines using only NATO airspace and land tartgets if necessary.

PAGE 2

FACTS: STRATEGIC AIRCRAFT CARRIERS:

United Kingdom has one aircraft carrier.

France has one air craft carrier.

United States has presently eleven commissioned aircraft carriers.

Italy has two.

Spain has one.

(A)   The presence of four aircraft carriers in international waters between

Norway and Denmark (NATO countries) as follows:

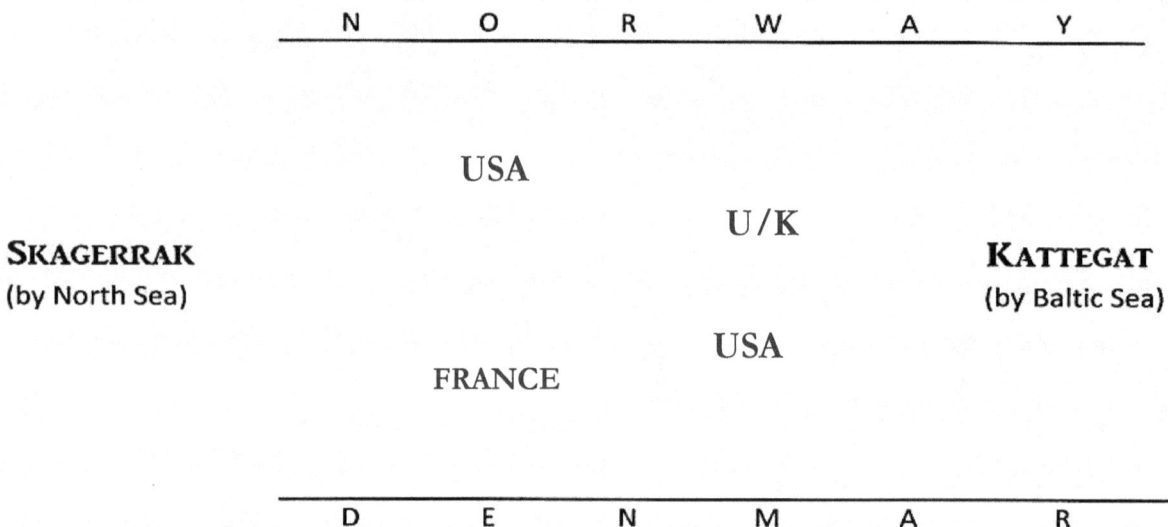

```
         N       O       R       W       A         Y

                     USA

                                   U/K

SKAGERRAK                                    KATTEGAT
(by North Sea)                               (by Baltic Sea)

                                    USA
                  FRANCE


         D       E       N       M       A       R       K
```

PAGE 3

B)   The presence of five NATO aircraft carries, in international waters, at the meeting of Dardanelles and the Aegean Sea is shown below. The formation of   *carriers*   provides greater safety than if stationed in the Sea of Marmara.

T   U   R   K   E   Y
_____

Italy   USA

AEGEAN SEA   Spain   **DARDANELLES**

Italy   USA

_____
T   U   R   K   E   Y

Exact location and utility of carriers, destroyers and accompanying nuclear submarine(s) would be determined by Naval Operations.

The presence of these ships is <u>not a blockade</u>, but a formation of Naval assets which will allow <u>all ships of any nation to pass threw, at will, without any interference what so ever from the five aircraft carriers and associated support ships.</u>

This is, impart, solely a NATO systems analysis and practice.

AIRCRAFT

Within a week, before the aircraft carrier formations form, the following NATO countries would each have four B-52 and four B1-B supersonic bombers from the United States and be located in strategic locations as directed by NATO:

Estonia	Poland
Latavia	Romania
Lithuania	Hungary

The aircraft in each country would be "grounded" until the two aircraft carrier fleets are fully in position. The stationing of the B-52 and B-1B bombers in the above countries constitutes 26% of the B-52 and B1-B arsenal and would not put the effectiveness of the US Air Force at risk. Additional "back-up"of aircraft in England, France and Germany may warrant publicized consideration by NATO.

The Russians must constantly be notified that the bombers are _not_ to be used aggressively and are solely a NATO "systems analysis and practice." In addition, emphasis must be placed upon a peaceful settlement of the Ukraine conflict without any casualities or military confrontations.

If an accord cannot be reached with the above formations of aircraft carriers and supersonic military aircraft the plan will continue as follows...

SUBMARINES

AND

<u>PEACEFUL</u> NON-NUCLEAR ICBM's

The concept of deploying <u>peaceful</u> ICBM's(non-nuclear), is to show a most concerning reaction by NATO to the prospects of war. Many considerations are relevant, some of which are presented below.

The use of conventional ICBM's would only be used as a <u>peaceful</u> means to deter the Russians from war. Each NATO country listed on the previous page would be a recipient of two conventional (non-nuclear) <u>peaceful</u> ICBM's from oceanic origins, directly to the respective NATO country (flight patterns over select NATO countries only). Target areas must be entirely isolated where there is no possibility of injury, death or destruction of productive physical property, by ICBM missiles.

ICBM action would begin once the two fleets are in position; all B-52 and B1-B bombers are in order. Submarines are at undisclosed locations and the receiving targets are prepared. The Russians must, must, must, be notified of the proposed <u>peaceful</u> ICBM plan, perhaps a week in advance and the day before commencement of the ICBM maneuvers. On day 1, two <u>peaceful</u> ICBM's would be launched into a predetermined NATO country and target two isolated landing areas. On day 2, two more <u>peaceful</u> ICBM missiles will be launched into a second NATO country, etc. Commencing on day 2, the first NATO country's ICBM target areas will be bombed twice a day by a B-52

PAGE 6

and a B1-B bomber. The daily bombings are scheduled to continue until the six country is bombed four times on the seventh day.

It is critical to note the launch methodology of the ICBM's used in the maneuvers. For example, a <u>peaceful</u> ICBM would be launched from the Baltic Sea directly into Poland and target a reasonable distance from the Ukraine boarder. Another <u>peaceful</u> ICBM from the North Atlantic Ocean over NATO countries France, Germany, Czech Republic into Poland and target a reasonable distance from the Ukraine boarder. Another example is launching a <u>peaceful</u> ICBM from the Adriatic Sea over NATO countries of Greece, Bulgaria into Romania and target a reasonable distance from the Ukraine boarder. The countries of Estonia, Latvia and Lithuania would be accessed directly from the Baltic Sea. The Russians must constantly be reinsured that NATO actions are <u>PEACEFUL</u> and within NATO boundaries and international waters. <u>Peaceful</u> ICBM flights over several NATO countries further personify those member countries of their commitment to NATO.

CASE STUDY:

MILITARY STRATEGY ASSESMENT

Assume four days have passed and the last B-52 and B1-B bombings have occurred for the day. The military plan has been progressing according to expectations with no interference by the Russians. Further, no negotiations for peace have occurred; however, economic sanctions have stabilized and the aspects for a deterrent are considered minimal.

As if you were Commander-in Chief of the entire U.S. armed forces, should there be change in the military plan at this point??? Full consideration must be given by yourself to continue NATO's efforts for a peaceful settlement of the NATO, Russian and Ukraine crisis. To that end, prepare a contingent plan to be considered by NATO. Formalize your plan in writing and exchange it with an acquaintance and debate your differences. The importance of your plan is that it will provide military planning insight to yourself, your debate, and given a chance, to your country!!!

PEACEFUL MILITARY DETERRENTS
AND
ECONOMIC SANCTIONS

Working togther, are to be used to offset the prospects of an aggressive WAR.

As previously noted:

There is no time to waste, to hold extensive deliberations or ignore the importance of human life and national sovereignty any further. NATO leadership has been cited as being weak and indecisive. Such a statement is true and must be rectified immediately, in my opinion. <u>A new leader must be given full command and responsibility of the NATO, Russian and Ukraine prospects of resolving potential warfare.</u>

<u>When man procrastinates, the ability to out manuever an enemy is abated.</u>

APPENDIX I

I HAD A DREAM, TOO

I HAD A DREAM, TOO

"I had a dream, too" chapter, written in Christopher's Book, portrays my concepts of an "INITIAL MEANS – TO-THE-END" solution in addressing the African holocaust. I purposely did not present pictures and statistics of various diseases inflicted to individuals such as those noted below, due to the graphic effects it my have on various age groups of my readers:

Pneumonia	HIV/AIDS virus
Diarrhea	Malaria
Tuberculosis	Measles
Whooping cough	Tetanus
Meningitis	Syphilis

The amount of deaths from the above diseases is unknown, but is estimated around ten million a year – a totally unconscionable amount for today's society. The majority of deaths occcur in children below the ages of five and are due from transmitted diseases and malnutrition.

One may ask, and rightfully so, why do Americans let this death toll exist and be accepted as a normal way of life? Apparently Americans would rather self medicate themselves with "Martinis and affluence" rather than face the fact that there is a holocaust existing in the world today. In Africa, there is just no excuse to allow murderous diseases to go unchecked and want for food withheld by the world on purpose. Why can't the United States share its purposely unplanted crops with the Africans? Will it become a known fact that Americans will not support the Musketeers who, given the opportunity, can solve in a relatively short period of time, Africa's future frontiers, where prosperity will be initially outlined and adhered to unil a country is healthy and operational?

Before I end, I cannot help but think of judgment day by GOD. A tough pill to swallow, will God forgive us to let millions of beautiful Africans die because of our affluence. Americans, like the Nazis, are killing –- <u>by not acting</u> — hundreds of millions of people over time out of <u>willful negligence</u>. I must warn Americans that monumental action must be taken to cure Africa or, as in the case of the Nazi's, be cast to hell.

Are we not placing the Africans in an environmental concentration camp, where death emanates to millions each year!!!

Oh Americans let's not forget Dr. Sperduto's last sermon when he stated we, through the Musketeers, must do what our Creator refuses to do. Why this is so? Why does God himself permit this? Something is morally wrong and it appears only man can rectify injustices to man. So be it!!!

APPENDIX II
ADVERSE DETERMINATION LETTER

DEPARTMENT OF HEALTH AND HUMAN SERVICES

Food and Drug Administration
Baltimore District Office
Central Region
6000 Metro Drive, Suite 101
Baltimore, MD 21215
Telephone: (410) 779-5455
FAX: (410) 779-5707

September 13, 2013

<u>ADVERSE DETERMINATION LETTER</u>

<u>BY ELECTRONIC & CERTIFIED MAIL
RETURN RECEIPT REQUESTED</u>

Mr. J. Chris Hrouda
Executive Vice President
Biomedical Services
American National Red Cross
2025 E Street, N.W.
Washington, D.C. 20006

RE: *United States v. American National Red Cross*, Civil Action No. 93-0949 (JGP)

Dear Mr. Hrouda:

From February 4 through March 1, 2013, United States Food and Drug Administration (FDA) investigators inspected American National Red Cross (ARC) Blood Services, Donor Management Center (Tulsa DMC facility), 2448 East 81st Street, Suite 2700, Tulsa, Oklahoma, and observed significant violations of the law, regulations, and the Amended Consent Decree of Permanent Injunction (Decree), entered on April 15, 2003[1]. At the conclusion of the inspection, the investigators issued a Form FDA 483, Inspectional Observations (FDA 483) on March 1, 2013, and an amended FDA 483 on March 28, 2013. The amended FDA 483 is attached (Attachment A). FDA is now, pursuant to Paragraph VIII of the Decree, notifying ARC of its determination that ARC has violated the Federal Food, Drug, and Cosmetic Act (the Act), FDA regulations, and the Decree, specifically Section 501(a)(2)(B) of the Act [21 U.S.C. § 351(a)(2)(B)], Title 21, Code of Federal Regulations (CFR) § 606, and Paragraphs IV.A and IV.B of the Decree. The violations include, but are not limited to, the following:

---

[1] FDA conducted the inspection of the Tulsa DMC facility in conjunction with inspections of three other ARC facilities where related objectionable conditions were also observed, specifically ARC's Heart of America Region, 405 W. John H. Gwynn Jr. Avenue, Peoria, IL. 61005 [7/10/2012 – 8/10/2012]; Southern California Region, 100 Red Cross Circle, Pomona, CA 91768 [7/10/2012 – 8/22/2012]; and the Donor and Client Support Center, 417 North Eighth Street, Philadelphia, PA 19123-3508 [9/5/2012 – 10/26/2012]. Copies of the FDA 483s issued at the conclusion of those inspections are included as Attachments B, C, and D, respectively.

GMP VIOLATIONS

Duplicate Donor Records[2]

1. Failure to have records available from which unsuitable donors may be identified so that products from such individuals will not be distributed **[21 CFR § 606.160(e)]**, and failure to maintain records that relate the donor with the unit number of each previous donation from that donor **[21 CFR § 606.160(b)(1)(vii)]**.

   Specifically, in preparation for the merger of ARC's National Donor Deferral Register (NDDR) and ARC's 36 regional National Biomedical Computer System (NBCS) databases into one national database known as eProgesa/BioArch Release 2.0 (hereafter, referred to as eProgesa)[3], ARC established three projects known as DMC 1, DMC 2, and DMC 3. The DMC 1 project was established in April 2006 primarily to resolve potential duplicate donor records without deferral assertions[4]; it was not established to resolve higher risk inter-regional duplicate donor records with deferral assertions recorded in a regional NBCS database or the NDDR[5]. The DMC 2 project, which was established in March 2010, was designed to resolve such records and to manage potentially unsuitable blood products, as appropriate. The DMC 3 project, which was established in July 2012, was designed to work concurrently with the DMC 2 project to resolve duplicate donor records other than those with inter-regional deferral assertions and refer those with assertions to the DMC 2. ARC delayed identification, investigation, and/or resolution of the potential duplicate donor records that presented the most risk of distribution of unsuitable blood products, specifically those involving donors who were indefinitely deferred in one of the regional NBCS databases and those involving donors who are permanently deferred in the NDDR. **[FDA 483 Observations 1 and 2.B]** For example,

   a. ARC paused the BioArch project from April 2008 through March 2010 to re-evaluate the implementation of eProgesa. During these two years, the DMC project did not investigate the thousands of already identified inter-regional duplicate donor records with known deferral assertions. Because duplicate donor records with deferral assertions present a potential for the release of unsuitable blood products, it is imperative that such records be promptly investigated and resolved. Each day these

---

[2] Decree paragraph III.B.33 defines duplicate donor records as "multiple donor records for the same donor which, because of inconsistent or duplicated information, may result in release for distribution of *unsuitable blood components.*"

[3] BioArch is a project which ARC is implementing in three stages: (1) BioArch Release 1 (R1), which upgraded the collections software solution and replaced collections equipment in the field; (2) BioArch Release 2 (R2), which replaced the NDDR and the regional NBCS databases with eProgesa; and (3) (b) (4) which has not been released.

[4] A deferral assertion is a code applied to a donor's record in ARC's computer system to ensure that the donor is identified as ineligible to donate blood products. Although ARC uses different terms to categorize deferrals such as indefinite and permanent, all deferrals entered into the NDDR are considered permanent.

[5] Inter-regional duplicate donor records are created when a donor donates in more than one region and has donation records in each of those regions. The NDDR contains records for all donors with specific categories of deferral assertions, such as Class X and surveillance class S assertion 99. In contrast, many other categories of donors who are deferred are only added to the NBCS database in the region where they are deemed ineligible to donate blood products. Whereas donor records with deferral assertions in the NDDR can be identified as deferred by all regions and thus distribution of unsuitable blood products from such donors can be prevented in the event of an inter-regional duplicate donor record, donors with a deferral in one of ARC's 36 regional NBCS databases are not included in the NDDR and cannot be identified by other regions as ineligible to donate blood products in the event of a duplicate donor record.

records are not resolved, the likelihood that unsuitable blood products being released for distribution increases.

b. ARC did not conduct the DMC projects in such a manner that placed a priority on identifying potentially unsuitable donors who were deferred in one region but subsequently donated in other regions. For instance, although ARC had the data needed to identify inter-regional duplicate donor records with NDDR Class X deferral assertions since April 2006, it did not design queries to identify such records and/or assign those cases to DMC 2 until November 2012, thereby significantly delaying the identification and investigation of unsuitable donors and the appropriate management of any unsuitable blood products. Instead, ARC prioritized DMC tasks on the basis of its internal implementation plans for eProgesa.

DECREE VIOLATIONS

Managerial Control and Duplicate Donor Records

2. Failure to comply with Decree paragraph IV.A which requires ARC to "take steps necessary to ensure continuous compliance with this Order, *the law*, and *ARC SOPs*, including but not limited to *BSDs*, *BSLs*, local operating procedures, and any other written instructions used by *ARC* in connection with the collection, manufacture, processing, packing, holding, or distribution of *blood* and *blood components*"; and failure to comply with Decree paragraph IV.B.6.b which requires that within 30 days of learning that a region failed to adequately investigate and completely correct duplicate donor records, ARC shall, "either (i) ensure that all such inadequately investigated or uncorrected records for the *region* have been reviewed and corrected, that all applicable *ARC SOPs* have been complied with, that all *unsuitable blood or blood components* have been identified and quarantined or retrieved...; or (ii) if such actions cannot be completed within the 30 *day* period, submit to FDA a written explanation for failure to meet that time-frame and implement a plan that establishes specific time-frames to complete each of the foregoing steps."

Specifically, in a June 20, 2008[6] letter to FDA, ARC stated that "[u]pon discovery of a donation from a donor who was deferred at one region and subsequently donated at another region, the donor has been entered into the National Donor Deferral Registry until donation eligibility has been clarified." However, FDA's review of ARC records found that the DMC projects had not and still does not follow this procedure. **[FDA 483 Observations 2.A and 5]** For example:

a. During the DMC 1 project, ARC identified thousands of inter-regional duplicate donor records with deferral assertions, but did not place those donors into the NDDR pending investigation of their suitability to donate blood products. It was not until the DMC 2 project began in March 2010 that ARC actively began investigating those cases.

---

[6] In its June 20, 2008 letter, ARC responded to concerns raised by FDA during a May 24, 2007, meeting between FDA and ARC pertaining to ARC's project to merge donor information in preparation for the implementation of the eProgesa computer system.

b. DMC 2 does not apply NDDR Class X deferral assertions to inter-regional duplicate donor records with deferral assertions in one region at the time they are identified, so that such donors will be recognized as ineligible to donate by other regions pending investigation of their suitability. Instead, DMC 2 applies the NDDR Class X deferral assertion only after the inter-regional duplicate donor records have been investigated and determined to be true duplicate records. Because the investigation process may take several months, ARC's failure to apply the NDDR Class X deferral assertion at the time the donor is identified may result in the distribution of unsuitable blood products if the donor is later confirmed to have true duplicate records with indefinite deferral assertions.

This list is not intended to be an all-inclusive list of deficiencies at your facilities. FDA has reviewed ARC's March 22, 2013, April 30, 2013, and June 28, 2013, responses to the Tulsa DMC FDA 483 and will verify promised corrective actions and evaluate their effectiveness during future inspections of ARC facilities.

* * *

ORDERS

Paragraph VIII of the Decree provides that "[i]n the event that FDA determines, based upon inspection...review of *ARC* records, or other information that comes to FDA's attention...that *ARC* is not following any *SOP* that may affect donor safety or the *purity* or labeling of *blood* or any *blood component*...; has violated *the law*; has failed to fully comply with any time frame, term, or provision of this Order...; then FDA may order *ARC* to come into compliance with *the law, ARC SOPs*, or this Order, assess penalties, and/or take any step that FDA deems necessary to bring *ARC* into compliance with *the law, ARC SOPs*, or this Order."

For the reasons stated above, FDA has determined that ARC did not comply with the law, ARC's SOPs, and the Decree. Therefore, FDA orders ARC to take the following actions:

1. Within 30 days of receipt of this letter and thereafter on a monthly basis, report to FDA, in writing, the status of ARC's progress towards investigating all inter-regional duplicate donor records. Such monthly reports shall continue until such time as FDA notifies ARC that the reports are no longer required. Each report should include the following:

   a. The number of cases that have been resolved between March 1, 2013 and the date of ARC's initial report under this Order. For all reports after the initial report, the report should include the number of cases resolved since the prior report, specifically identifying the number of cases involving inter-regional duplicate donor records with assertions;

   b. The number of cases pending and the number of cases in-process, specifically identifying for each the number of cases involving inter-regional duplicate donor records with assertions;

c. The number of unsuitable blood products that were retrieved from subsequent donations each month;

2. Within 30 days of receipt of this letter, provide FDA ARC's written schedule for identifying and updating the population of inter-regional duplicate donors that require investigation by the DMC project.

* * *

For the reasons stated above, FDA has determined that ARC did not comply with the law, ARC SOPs, and the Decree. Although FDA regards the violations discussed in this letter to be significant and could have assessed penalties as in previous Adverse Determination Letters issued to the ARC under paragraph IX of the Decree, we are notifying you of the violations that we found so that you can take appropriate action to address them and comply with the orders set forth above. If FDA determines that ARC is not complying with the above stated orders, FDA will reevaluate assessing penalties or consider an alternate or additional regulatory measure.

As provided in Paragraph IX of the Decree, if ARC agrees with this adverse determination, it must within 20 days of receipt of this letter, notify FDA of its agreement. If ARC disagrees with FDA's adverse determination, it must respond in writing within 20 days of receipt of this letter, explaining its reasons for disagreeing with FDA's determination. Your response must be submitted to me at the Food and Drug Administration, Baltimore District Office, 6000 Metro Drive, Suite 101, Baltimore, Maryland 21215, with a copy to Karen Midthun, M.D., Director, Center for Biologics Evaluation and Research, 1401 Rockville Pike, Suite 200N, Rockville, Maryland 20852.

Sincerely yours,

Evelyn Bonnin
Director, Baltimore District

Enclosures

cc: Gail McGovern
President and Chief Executive Officer
American National Red Cross
2025 E Street, N.W.
Washington, D.C. 20006

Kathryn Waldman
Senior Vice President
  for Quality and Regulatory Affairs
American National Red Cross
2025 E Street, N.W.
Washington, D.C. 20006

David Meltzer
General Counsel
American National Red Cross
2025 E Street, N.W.
Washington, D.C. 20006

Bonnie McElveen-Hunter
Chairman, Board of Governors
American National Red Cross
2025 E Street, N.W.
Washington, D.C. 20006

APPENDIX III

STATE OF NEW JERSEY

Ode

to

the

<u>State of New Jersey</u>

<u>Department of Human Services</u>

My *pension* is imperative.

My *medical plan* is indespensible in sustaining my life.

My new career as an author is a direct result of your support over the years and standing by me when the going got tuff as an financial auditor. Accept for the end, I will always be thankful…

Christopher

www.ingramcontent.com/pod-product-compliance
Lightning Source LLC
LaVergne TN
LVHW081314060426
835509LV00015B/1511